PREGNANCY & EXERCISE

PREGNANCY & EXERCISE

Artal Mittelmank, Raul

RAUL ARTAL, M.D.

WITH

GENELL J. SUBAK-SHARPE

DELACORTE PRESS

This book is dedicated to
our daughters

Published by
Delacorte Press
Bantam Doubleday Dell Publishing Group, Inc.
666 Fifth Avenue
New York, New York 10103

Before attempting any exercises in this book, the pregnant woman is advised to consult with her physician or obstetrician.

Design: Stanley S. Drate/Folio Graphics Co., Inc.

Library of Congress Cataloging in Publication Data

Artal Mittelmark, Raul.
  Pregnancy and exercise : a complete program for women before and
after giving birth / by Raul Artal ; with Genell J. Subak-Sharpe.
    p. cm.
  ISBN 0-385-30120-0
  1. Pregnancy. 2. Exercise for women. I. Subak-Sharpe, Genell J.
II. Title.
RG558.7.A67 1992
618.2′4—dc20   91-46768
                                                           CIP

Manufactured in the United States of America
Published simultaneously in Canada

August 1992

10 9 8 7 6 5 4 3 2 1

RRH

CONTENTS

v

1

WHEN TODAY'S WOMAN HAS A BABY

In my twenty-two years of practicing obstetrics, I have been privileged to witness two revolutions in pregnancy and childbirth. One
revolution centers on today's advanced medical technology and our
increased scientific understanding of reproduction. Thanks to this technology, for example, thousands of previously infertile couples can now
experience the joys of parenthood. Women with diseases such as diabetes or high blood pressure now deliver normal, healthy babies. And
we are now able to save premature babies that weigh barely 500 grams
(a little over a pound)—a feat that was impossible just a few years ago.

The second revolution rests with today's woman and the way that
she and her partner approach pregnancy, childbirth, and parenthood.
This revolution may be less tangible than the technological one, but it is
just as real, and it has certainly changed the practice of obstetrics. Not

long ago it was the doctor who "called the shots" throughout the pregnancy, even dictating when and how a baby would be born. Typically, the mother would be put to sleep with a general anesthetic and, while the father paced the halls, the obstetrician would deliver the baby. The newborn would then be whisked away to a nursery and cared for by a team of nurses. If the mother elected to breast-feed (most did not, even twenty years ago), the baby would be brought to her on a specific schedule. The father and other family members were often barred from holding or even being in the same room with the baby; instead, they viewed the infant through protective glass. Even though I was an obstetrician, I was not allowed to witness the birth of my first child! The field of obstetrics has obviously changed a great deal since then.

This began to change in the 1960s, with such "revolutionary" concepts as rooming in, with the mother assuming at least part of the care of the newborn; and natural or partner-assisted labor and delivery, with the father as an active participant in the birth process. Actually, many of the changes were simply an updating of past practices, when most babies were born at home and cared for by the mother and other family members.

Today, the woman (usually along with her partner) makes the final decisions, with the obstetrician as the medical adviser and helper. Granted, some physicians complain that the pendulum has swung too far and that they have been relegated to the role of a technician. However, most—including myself—applaud the changes. I strongly feel that the woman should be given all the facts and that the final decision as to what happens to her and her baby should be hers to make. The obstetrician is an informed partner, helper, and teacher, with a vast array of technological advances to help obtain a healthy outcome for both the mother and baby. He or she is there to provide guidelines, support, and medical intervention if it's needed. But it's the woman herself who now plays the leading role and is the star of the show!

Obviously, with today's woman assuming the responsibility for making so many decisions that were once the exclusive province of the doctor, it's vital that she and her partner be as fully informed as possible. Typically, today's pregnant woman combines a career with pregnancy and parenthood. She is also more physically active than women in the past. Pregnancies, for the most part, are carefully planned, with a renewed focus on health and fitness even before conception takes place. Many of my patients come to me before pregnancy seeking advice on diet, medication, exercise, and health habits. Their goal is to ensure a healthy pregnancy from the very beginning. Often, this is a time for the entire family to take stock of health habits and to alter those that are detrimental. For example, I encounter many fathers who stop smoking during their wives' pregnancies, saying they are doing so "to provide a healthy environment for my baby."

Many of my patients are elite athletes, and maintaining their competitive athletic status is one of their major concerns. But they also want to know about nutrition, possible occupational hazards, and numerous other aspects of pregnancy and childbirth. I also have many women referred to me who are at high risk for pregnancy loss. These women are perhaps even more concerned about the effects of life-style on their pregnancies. The common refrain I hear from both groups is: "Doctor, I don't want to be an invalid for the next nine months, but I do want a healthy baby."

My goal in writing this book has been to offer the general guidelines for exercise during pregnancy that have evolved from the research and medical experience of myself and my colleagues. Throughout, we stress that these are only guidelines—there's no single right way, and what is best for one woman is not necessarily so for another. I strongly support the concept that the woman should have the final say. The information in this book is intended to help in this decision-making. It should not, however, supplant the advice of your own obstetrician, who knows your personal health background and can help you in your own decision-making process.

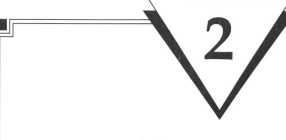

PREGNANCY AND CHILDBIRTH

A Historic Perspective

Throughout history, women have been given all sorts of advice on how best to deal with pregnancy and childbirth. These advisers have ranged from physicians and midwives to some of our greatest philosophers and statesmen.

As might be expected, a good deal of this advice has centered on physical activity during pregnancy. Early on, observers correlated an uneventful pregnancy and easy labor with physical activity. In the third century B.C., for example, Aristotle attributed difficult childbirth to a sedentary life-style. In Exodus, Chapter 1, Verse 19, the Biblical writers observed that the Hebrew slave women had an easier time giving birth than their Egyptian mistresses: ". . . the Hebrew women are not as the Egyptian women; for they are lively, and are delivered ere the midwives come in unto them."

As early physicians and midwives gained an increased understanding of the physical processes involved, women were given more precise advice regarding exercise during pregnancy. By the eighteenth century, physicians generally supported the notion that physical activity during pregnancy was beneficial. In 1788 James Lucas, a surgeon at the Leeds General Infirmary in England, presented a paper to the Medical Society of London in which he advocated exercise during pregnancy, on the premise that exercise would result in a smaller baby that would pass more easily through the birth canal. Still, there were dissenters, and many physicians felt that pregnancy should be a time of rest and confinement.

■ *A More Restrictive View*

In the New World this more restrictive view was gaining popularity. Alexander Hamilton, in his 1781 *Treatise of Midwifery*, outlined a set of "Rules and Cautions for the Conduct of Pregnant Women," in which he urged only moderate activities. In particular, he cautioned women to avoid "agitation of the body from violent or improper exercise, as jolting in a carriage, riding on horseback, dancing and whatever disturbs the body or mind."

During the Victorian era an even more confining and paternalistic view toward women and what was fitting and healthy prevailed. One of the popular books of the day was entitled *Married Lady's Companion and Poor Man's Friend* by Samuel K. Jennings. By today's standards Jennings's advice is often the opposite of what is considered medically valid.

"It is common opinion," he wrote, "that breeding women ought to live indolently and feast luxuriously as they are able, lest by exercise they should injure, or by abstinence debilitate the unborn child. Those ladies who are accustomed to idleness and who, of course, cannot take any considerable degree of exercise without consequent soreness or even fever, ought by no means to indulge in riding on horseback, running or romping, in any stage of pregnancy."

His advice was far different for the less privileged laboring class. For them, he advised: "The happier class of women, who are in the habit of daily labor and continued exercise, may continue their engagements as before, except only, that it may be necessary to abate from their common fatigue in a gradual manner, as they advance in pregnancy. If, however, any of the symptoms threatening danger should present themselves, a little blood should be drawn from the arm and repeated as often as necessary."

To the Victorian lady, the confinement of pregnancy was just that. It was considered unseemly for a pregnant woman to engage in social activities or to even be seen outside her family setting.

∎ Early Scientific Studies

Until the late nineteenth century, most of the medical and public attitudes regarding exercise and pregnancy were based largely on personal observations. In 1895 the first scientific study on the subject was published. This study reviewed the outcomes of one thousand pregnancies, drawing a relationship among a high level of maternal physical activity, low birth weight, and increased perinatal mortality. A similar study by a French physician named Letourneur was published in 1896. This research reviewed 627 deliveries in Paris and observed that intense physical labor, especially during the latter part of pregnancy, had a greater effect on whether the woman would have an undersized baby than whether she was thin. A Viennese physician found that women who rested a good deal during pregnancy had larger babies and a lower infant mortality rate than their more active peers. In retrospect, these studies served to confirm what writers since Aristotle had observed, namely that intense physical activity, especially near the end of pregnancy, resulted in smaller than average babies.

These early scientific studies were soon correlated with declining health of the population as a whole. In the early years of the twentieth century a number of writers decried the generally poor health of military recruits. In England, for example, it was estimated that only forty percent of male volunteers were healthy enough for military service. British politicians were quick to denounce the "declining quality of the British population." And where did the blame lie? The politicians of the day faulted the fact that more and more women were working in factories, including during pregnancy. Before long, several countries, including England, Holland, Belgium, Portugal, Austria, and Switzerland adopted laws prohibiting pregnant women from working in factories in the two to four weeks before childbirth and up to six weeks afterward.

■ A Theme of Moderation

Such laws were not passed in the United States, but moderation was becoming a common theme. A 1913 handbook for pregnant women advised: "Walking is the best kind of exercise. Most women who are pregnant find that a two- to three-mile walk daily is all they enjoy, and very few are inclined to indulge in six miles, which is generally accepted as the upper limit. Very few outdoor sports can be unconditionally recommended to the prospective mother. Because athletic exercise is either too violent or else jolts the body a great deal, it is especially dangerous in the early months of pregnancy. All kinds of violent exertion should be avoided—a rule which at once excludes sweeping, scrubbing, laundry work, lifting anything that is heavy, and going up and down stairs hurriedly or frequently. The use of a sewing machine is also emphatically forbidden."

By 1935 even more precautions were added. To quote from *Modern Motherhood*, one of the more popular guides of the day: "The expectant mother must, of necessity, curtail her usual physical activities because of her extra burden. She cannot exercise more than she is accustomed to; she should exercise less. She should not be persuaded to walk a lot [even though] walking is supposed to make birth easier—this superstition is hundreds of years old and still prevalent."

■ Exercises for Childbirth Preparation

During the 1920s and 1930s the first prenatal exercise programs were developed, with the objectives of easing childbirth and reducing the need for pain medication. Exercise training for childbirth became popular in both the United States and Europe. An American, Dr. G. D. Read, developed breathing and physical exercises aimed at reducing the pain of childbirth. A Russian named Velvovsky developed a regimen for "painless" childbirth, which was introduced to the West in the late 1950s by Ferdinand Lamaze. That program is now called the Lamaze Method. The notion of "natural childbirth" was initially designated for uncomplicated, nonoperative home deliveries. It was only later on that the term "natural childbirth" was used to describe labor in the absence of analgesics. This description was quickly adopted by Lamaze program instructors and subsequently tied in to exercise.

By the 1940s and 1950s the pendulum again swung in favor of moderate exercise. In 1949 the U.S. Children's Bureau recommended: "A moderate amount of exercise is good for anyone, and this is particularly true for pregnant woman. Unless you have been ill or unless there is some complication, you can continue your housework, gardening, daily walks, and even swim occasionally."

■ The Fitness Boom

The great fitness boom of the 1970s quickly extended itself to pregnancy. Both men and women took up vigorous sports such as running, competitive swimming, racquetball, and long-distance bicycling. By the 1980s, "go for the burn" became something of a rallying cry, and exercise promoters promised everything from a longer life to increased sexual prowess and youthfulness.

Pregnant women were encouraged to join a rash of special aerobic-exercise programs and classes. Not uncommonly, the promises went beyond demonstrated benefits. One popular book, *Exercise Plus Pregnancy Program,* claims that "successfully completing an exercise program will give you a greater sense of control over your body. Being in control, while at the same time being relaxed, will give you the confidence and trust you'll need to 'let go' for a smoother labor and delivery." In addition to engaging in various exercise programs, a growing number of women held jobs outside the home. Many of these were in fields heretofore closed to women: construction, fire fighting, truck driving, among many others. Experts began to question whether the pendulum had again swung too far. Was it really safe for a pregnant woman to "go for the burn"?

▪ *Promises vs. Scientific Data*

Despite the many promises and perceived benefits of exercise during pregnancy, until recently there has been very little scientific data to either substantiate or refute these claims. Heretofore, medical researchers have had little or no scientific evidence on how various types of exercise affect the fetus and the pregnant woman. How much exercise is desirable? And how much is too much? Are some exercises better than others? How can today's active woman continue her life-style without jeopardizing herself or her baby? These are among the many questions that are addressed on the following pages. We certainly don't claim to have all the answers, but our research has provided important new insight. One of the major objectives of this book is to present the scientific evidence and to offer readers guidelines they can use in maintaining an active, healthy pregnancy.

3

THE EFFECTS OF EXERCISE ON THE REPRODUCTIVE SYSTEM

It is now well established that exercise can have profound effects on well advised to participate in a sound fitness program that incorporates regular, moderate exercise can improve circulation, help control weight, tone flabby muscles, improve posture, aid in sleep, and promote a sense of well-being, all of which can help you maintain a normal life-style while experiencing a healthy pregnancy. Also, moderate exercise can help you get back in shape after pregnancy.

Conversely, too much rigorous exercise or the wrong kind of regimen—for example, such activities as competitive swimming or training for a marathon—can overstress your body and may even prevent you from being able to conceive. Specifically, overly rigorous exercise in some women can lead to the cessation of the menstrual cycle, a condition known as amenorrhea, or an infrequent or irregular cycle, known as oligomenorrhea.

■ *How Exercise Affects Ovulation*

Medical research reveals that women who participate in strenuous physical training often skip several periods or stop menstruating altogether. A 1978 article in *Lancet*, a British medical journal, described amenorrhea in a group of athletes. The researchers, led by Dr. C. B. Feicht, found that twenty percent of women who ran twenty miles a week stopped menstruating. And the more they ran, the greater the effect. Among those who ran seventy to eighty miles per week, the percentage of women who ceased menstruating more than doubled, rising to forty-three percent.

Another study, this one conducted by Dr. S. F. Abraham and colleagues and reported in the British *Journal of Obstetrics and Gynecology* in 1982, found that seventy-nine percent of young women ballet dancers involved in rigorous dance training had stopped menstruating or at least experienced irregular periods.

Researchers believe that more than one factor contributes to these menstrual disturbances, but weight and percentage of body fat are two important factors. Studies show, for example, that young girls begin to add body fat with the onset of puberty. Overweight girls are likely to begin menstruating earlier than their normal-weight peers. Similarly, very thin girls with a low percentage (less than fifteen percent) of body fat are likely to start menstruating later than average. Even after the onset of menstruation the excessive loss of weight and body fat may cause menstruation to cease. Thus, low body weight, which often occurs in physically active individuals who expend more energy through strenuous exercise than they are taking in through food, may hinder a woman's attempts to conceive because of hormonal responses that can disrupt the reproductive cycle.

Even if you have sufficient body weight, too much exercise still can alter the regulatory mechanisms of the reproductive centers in your brain. Once these mechanisms are thrown off kilter they cause hormonal changes and imbalances that can disburb the entire reproductive cycle and prevent you from being able to become pregnant (see box, "The Case of Lisa T.").

Lisa T. is a twenty-seven-year-old schoolteacher who started running when she was in college. Recently she decided she was ready to run a marathon and began intensive training with the track coach at the school where she teaches. During a typical week Lisa would run twelve to fifteen miles each morning, and on Saturday she and her coach would run twenty to twenty-five miles.

Heretofore, Lisa had menstruated regularly, but after six weeks of this rigorous training she missed a period. She knew this often happened when embarking on a competitive training program, so she was not concerned. But when she failed to have a period during the next month, she started to wonder if she was overdoing it. In addition to competing in a marathon, Lisa's future plans included starting a family. In fact, she and her husband had decided to try to achieve a pregnancy in the months following the race.

Even though Lisa was running some eighty miles a week, she had not lost weight, and in fact she weighed a couple of pounds more than she had when she began her marathon training. She waited one more month, and when she again failed to menstruate she made an appointment to see her doctor.

Although Lisa's weight was normal for her height (she was five feet seven inches and she weighed 137 pounds), her doctor used a pair of calipers (instruments that measure skin folds) to estimate her percentage of body fat. This test indicated that only eight or nine percent of her weight was body fat, far less than the fifteen to twenty percent that is normal for a woman of her age. Muscle and bone weigh more than fat. Thus, Lisa's well-developed muscles and bone structure accounted for the fact that her weight registered in the normal range, even though her percentage of body fat was too low.

Lisa's physical examination, which included a pelvic exam, was normal. But to make sure that her amenorrhea was not due to other causes, Lisa's doctor ordered a few tests. The initial test ordered was prolactin—a hormone secreted in the pituitary that affects milk production. High levels of prolactin may alert to the possibility of a pituitary tumor and are frequently associated with amenorrhea.

When prolactin returned normal, her estrogen status was evaluated by injecting her with progesterone. She was supposed to menstruate after the injection, but she did not, indicating that her serum estradiol (a biologically active estrogen) was too low. Estrogen replacement was necessary.

Lisa was then given a choice: She could cut back on her running to see if this would restore her normal menstrual cycle. Alternatively, the doctor could prescribe hormone-replacement therapy, which would help prevent premature osteoporosis—a thinning of the bone that occurs with aging and is particularly common in postmenopausal women who no longer produce estrogen.

Lisa elected to take the hormones, at least until she had fulfilled her ambition to compete in the marathon. After that, she planned to cut back on her running and to eat more to increase her percentage of body fat. Once her normal menstrual cycle resumed, she would start on her second objective—having a baby.

■ *How the Reproductive Cycle Works*

In order to understand why and how exercise and hormonal disruptions can prevent pregnancy, it's important to have a clear picture of how the reproductive system works (see Figure 1). Several hormonal phases comprise your menstrual cycle. Each phase is controlled by signals that originate in the hypothalamic section of the brain.

On the first day of your menstrual cycle, which is the first day of bleeding, the hypothalamus signals the pituitary gland to send out follicle-stimulating hormone (FSH). Under the influence of FSH, several eggs, called ova, start to develop in the ovaries. As they develop they produce estrogen, which is sent out into the bloodstream.

Although each egg contains forty-six chromosomes at this stage, it must reduce its nuclear contents to twenty-three chromosomes in order to be fertilized by a sperm. To achieve this, each egg, or ovum, divides and spins off twenty-three chromosomes into a duplicate cell, called a polar body, while keeping the remaining twenty-three for itself. Eventually the polar body shrivels up and becomes useless, although it continues to travel alongside the vital egg.

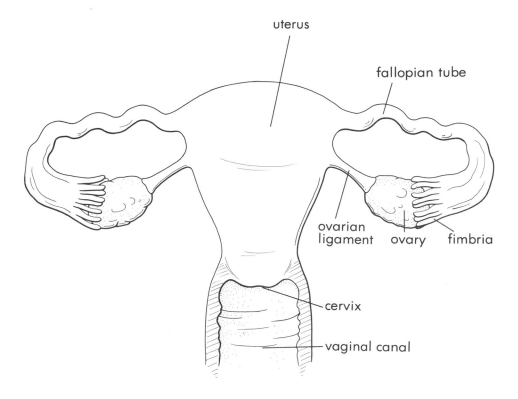

Fig. 1. Normal female reproductive organs

Meanwhile, one egg of the many that are developing begins to grow faster than the others. Its outside shell thickens and separates into four layers. The two inside layers offer tight protection for the egg, while the two outside layers balloon away from it and the sac fills with fluid.

The typical twenty-eight-day menstrual cycle is controlled by a complex interplay of hormones. (In reality, very few women have regular twenty-eight-day cycles. The normal menstrual cycle ranges from twenty to forty days, with the mean being twenty-five to thirty days.) In general, the menstrual cycle can be divided into five distinct phases.

PHASE 1 (DAYS 1–5)

Menstruation. Each cycle is timed from the onset of menstruation, which may actually last from three to seven days. During menstruation, estrogen (the hormone that controls ovulation) and progesterone (the hormone that prepares the body for pregnancy) fall to their lowest levels, which signals the master controls in the brain—the pituitary and hypothalamus—to step up production of LH (luteinizing hormone) and FSH. Both of these are stimulating hormones and their rise signals the ovaries that it is time to begin a new cycle. Specifically, LH stimulates the ovaries to secrete more estrogen, and FSH stimulates a follicle within one of the ovaries to begin "ripening" a new egg.

PHASE 2 (DAYS 6–12)

The follicular stage. During this time, levels of both estrogen and LH continue to rise. When estrogen reaches a specific high point it signals the pituitary to reduce its secretion of FSH; at the same time, the rising estrogen levels stimulate the pituitary to pump out even more LH.

PHASE 3 (DAYS 12–13)

The proliferative stage. At this time there is a surge of estrogen, which prompts a sharp rise in LH, which in turn causes a rise in FSH.

PHASE 4 (DAY 14)

Ovulation. The surge of LH prompts the follicle to release its egg and ovulation takes place. The ovum, now called the graafian follicle, reaches a bursting point, bulging out on the surface of the ovary. At this stage, high levels of estrogen circulate in the bloodstream. The rise in estrogen is detected by the hypothalamus in the brain, which signals the pituitary gland to secrete LH. This hormone weakens the wall of the follicle and causes it to collapse. When the egg is released, ovulation occurs. The mature egg enters the fallopian tube and begins its journey to the uterus. This is the precise time during the menstrual cycle in

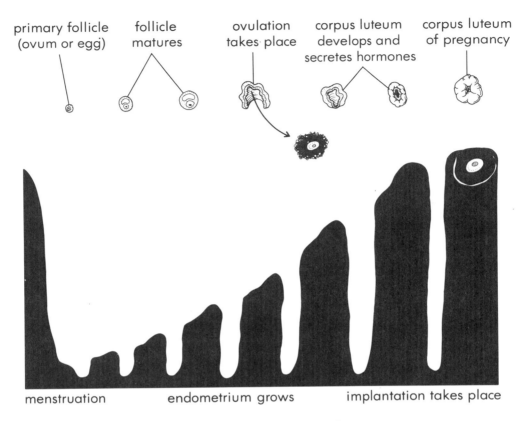

primary follicle
(ovum or egg)

follicle
matures

ovulation
takes place

corpus luteum
develops and
secretes hormones

corpus luteum
of pregnancy

menstruation   endometrium grows   implantation takes place

Fig. 2. Normal ovulation, fertilization, and implantation.
The above schematic shows a menstrual cycle in which fertilization and
implantation take place, thereby establishing a pregnancy.

which conception can occur if the male sperm joins with the mature egg
in the fallopian tube.

PHASE 5 (DAYS 15–27)

The luteal phase. This second half of the cycle is called the luteal phase.
This is the time when progesterone, another female hormone, takes
over. After the ruptured ovarian follicle releases its ripened egg, it
becomes the corpus luteum (the small, yellowish structure that produces progesterone during the luteal phase). With the rise in progesterone, LH and FSH drop to their lowest levels of the menstrual

cycle. The rising progesterone has a profound effect on the lining of the uterus (the endometrium). It thickens and becomes engorged with blood. These changes are in anticipation of establishing a pregnancy. If conception takes place within a day or two of ovulation, the uterus must be prepared to receive the fertilized egg and begin to provide the nourishment it will need to grow into a viable fetus. From day 15 to about day 22, the endometrium more than doubles in thickness.

If conception does not occur, on about day 22 or 23 the corpus luteum begins to shrink and progesterone secretion falls. This drop causes the endometrium to begin to break down—a process that occupies the last five or six days of the cycle. The blood vessels shrink, depriving the uterine lining of its blood supply. Pieces of the lining begin to fall away and the weakened blood vessels open, discharging droplets of blood. This menstrual flow empties the uterus. On day 28 (or fourteen days from the time of ovulation) menstruation starts, beginning a new cycle.

■ If Fertilization Takes Place

Of course, the scenario just described is much different if fertilization takes place just after ovulation (see Fig. 2). After its release from the matured follicle the egg seems to suspend itself in space and then moves on to the opening of the fallopian tube, where it is drawn inside by millions of cilia, hairlike cells that carry the egg toward the uterus. It is only when the egg is in the high reaches of the tube, where it remains for about twelve to twenty-four hours, that the egg can be fertilized (providing, of course, that there is also sperm in the tube).

The egg next moves through the fallopian tube and is deposited in the uterus. If it has been fertilized it clings to the inside wall and nourishes itself in the endometrium. The fertilized egg begins to produce the pregnancy hormone, human chorionic gonadotropin (hCG), which signals the brain and pituitary gland to continue sending LH to the endometrium so that the fertilized egg can develop into a fetus. The corpus luteum continues to produce hormones that promote development of the placenta, which in turn pumps out pregnancy hormones.

Even though this is a somewhat simplified description of the menstrual cycle, you can readily see that it involves a complex interplay of hormones and other factors. Each stage of the reproductive cycle must occur if you are to become pregnant. Although there is considerable variation among individuals, most women menstruate fairly regularly once their pattern of ovulation has been established during puberty. Although it is possible to have a period without ovulating, and vice versa, in most instances the cessation of regular periods generally signals that something has changed in the reproductive cycle and that pregnancy may not be achieved.

▪ *The Negative Effects of Strenuous Exercise*

As mentioned earlier, research reveals that women involved in unusually rigorous exercise, such as young ballet dancers and competitive athletes who undergo strenuous physical training, often stop having their periods or, in some cases, menstruate infrequently. It appears, then, that exercise can cause disturbances in normal menstrual cycles (amenorrhea or oligomenorrhea). In many instances these disruptions can be traced to changes that occur in the mechanisms that regulate the reproductive centers in the brain. These changes modify the production and release of the various hormones that play so integral a part in the reproductive cycle. (It should also be noted that stress plays an important role, independent of exercise, in bringing about these changes. For example, a competitive athlete or professional dancer may resume normal menstrual cycles after stopping professional appearances, even though the total physical activity or body composition may be unchanged.)

In recent years we have learned a good deal about the mechanisms involved in the interplay of exercise and the menstrual cycle. For example, studies show that when you exercise vigorously your body releases beta-endorphins, in conjunction with the release of ACTH (one of the "stress" hormones produced by the adrenal glands), as a response to this physical exertion. While these endorphins often are credited with triggering a "feel-good" response in most individuals, they also serve to inhibit the release of gonadotropins, the hormones that stimulate the ovaries to carry out their reproductive functions. If the hormones that make ovulation possible are suppressed, pregnancy obviously cannot occur. Similarly, the uterus does not go through its cyclic changes, and menstruation will not take place (see box, "The Case of Mary L.").

■ THE CASE OF MARY L.

Mary L. is a twenty-four-year-old ballerina who recently was picked to fill out the ballet season for a performer who suffered a broken leg. It was the sort of "big break" that Mary had dreamed about but had not really expected to happen. Suddenly, instead of spending several hours each day in practice sessions, Mary found herself onstage for three or four performances each week.

Until this time Mary had menstruated regularly. She knew that many of her colleagues did not have regular periods. She attributed her normal menstrual function to the fact that she made sure her food intake was enough to maintain a normal weight. Hence, she was surprised when she failed to have a period during the first month of her performances. The ballet company's consulting physician assured her that this often happened and that she should not worry. But the same thing happened during the next two months.

The season then ended, and Mary resumed her former schedule of daily lessons and occasional performances. Although she had loved her months in the spotlight, Mary was also somewhat relieved to be free of the stress of regular performances. At the same time, her menstrual periods returned. Although her level of physical activity was unchanged, the reduction in stress was enough to prompt her body to again function normally.

Another problem revealed by recent research concerns pituitary function. Normally, luteinizing hormone (LH), which in the luteal phase influences the corpus luteum to release the progesterone that helps support and build the endometrium, is regulated by the pituitary. But when you exercise strenuously, the body's level of progesterone increases independently of the pituitary, which disturbs the normal stages of the reproductive cycle. The result is that this hormonal imbalance will make it difficult, if not impossible, for you to become pregnant.

Of course, every women reacts differently to exercise, and what may be too much for you may be just right for someone else. But in general, studies report that whatever your fitness levels, overly rigorous exercise stresses your body and changes its hormonal functioning seriously enough to disrupt the stages of the normal reproductive cycle, leading to menstrual abnormalities.

Normal ovulation and reproductive function depend upon a woman having a certain amount of body fat. A marked loss of weight and reduction of body fat will disrupt normal ovulation—at least for a time. Thus, strenuous exercise regimens that emphasize low body weight may lead to poor nutrition and/or the consumption of too few calories. In turn, this can result in menstrual irregularities or the cessation of your period and ovulation.

Even in cases where your period has completely stopped, such exercise-induced (or exercise- and stress-induced) infertility is almost always reversible if you curtail the rigorous exercise program that may have caused the problems in the first place. That is, once your body is no longer under excessive physical stress, the hormonal balance seems to be restored, leading to the resumption of a regular menstrual cycle. If you had become too thin, but have now regained sufficient body fat, your periods usually will resume also. (Note: Poor nutrition and low weight gain prior to and during pregnancy carry an increased risk of having an undersized baby—a fairly common occurrence among women who exercise and fail to eat enough to support both pregnancy and their physical activity.) It should be emphasized that a very muscular woman may carry a seemingly adequate number of pounds, but still have inadequate body fat. For example, one of my patients—a competitive cyclist—weighed 125 pounds, which was in the normal range for her height of five feet five inches. But less than ten percent of her weight was body fat. Remember, muscle and bone weigh more than fat; thus a muscular, heavy-boned five-foot five-inch woman may weigh 140 pounds or more and not be overly fat. In contrast, a fine-boned woman of the same height who is in poor physical condition with underdeveloped muscles may look fat and flabby at the same weight.

It is important to understand that when periods resume they usually do so with the same regularity they had prior to their cessation. That is, if your periods were irregular prior to the exercise regimen that caused them to stop, they most likely will be irregular once they begin again. Likewise, if they were regular before they stopped, they probably will be regular when they resume.

If you are planning on becoming pregnant, therefore, you would be well advised to participate in a sound fitness program that incorporates moderate, but not overly strenuous, exercise.

■ *Safety Guidelines for Prepregnancy Exercise*

We are living in a health-conscious era in which more and more women are participating in all forms of sports and exercise. As long as you don't overdo it, establishing and/or continuing a moderate exercise regimen will serve you well when you become pregnant, increasing your strength and stamina, keeping you energized, and boosting your self-esteem. Excessive exercise may ultimately lead to injuries that will prevent you from engaging in any physical activity, thus defeating the very goal for which you have aimed. In our practice we urge women to follow the general guidelines from the American College of Obstetricians and Gynecologists and the American College of Sports Medicine, which are summarized below:

Frequency of training—three to five days a week.

Intensity of training—sixty to ninety percent of maximum heart rate (220 beats per minute minus your age).

Duration of sessions: twenty to sixty minutes of continuous aerobic activity.

Type of activity: any that uses large muscles and that can be maintained continuously, is rhythmic, and aerobic. Examples include walking, hiking, running/jogging, cycling, stationary cycling, cross-country skiing, dancing, rope skipping, rowing, stair climbing, swimming, skating, and various endurance games. Resistance machines for strength training should involve small weights sufficient to develop and maintain muscles. For example, eight to twelve repetitions of eight to ten exercises that condition major muscle groups should be performed at least twice a week.

▪ *Practical Tips to Get Started*

The following tips for prepregnancy exercise conditioning will help get you in shape without overstressing your body or disrupting your menstrual cycle:

- If you are out of shape, begin exercising slowly with some low-impact, low-intensity activity like walking, swimming, or cycling and build up your exercise level gradually.
- Wear proper exercise clothing, including a support bra and good athletic shoes that cushion any impact.
- Eventually, strive to exercise fifteen to twenty minutes every day or moderately twenty to thirty minutes three times a week. These shorter, regular exercise periods are better for you than exercising for an hour or so once a week; intermittent exercise can strain muscles, joints, and ligaments.
- Unless you are substantially overweight, don't go on a weight-reduction diet in an effort to compensate for the weight you'll gain during your pregnancy. Any sharp drop in body fat can upset your hormonal balance and make it more difficult for you to conceive. Right now it's

more important to concentrate on exercise that builds your stamina, endurance, muscle strength, and your cardiovascular capacity.

■ Choose an exercise regimen that you can continue into your pregnancy. This is not the time to take up a new and highly demanding or potentially dangerous sport like scuba diving or skydiving, which should be curtailed during pregnancy. Walking, swimming, and cycling are good choices before and during pregnancy, because they help firm muscles and improve circulation without causing any undue stress.

■ If you are already involved in heavy weight-bearing exercises like weight lifting or rock climbing, switch to more moderate activities like walking, swimming, and working with a stationary bicycle.

■ Steer clear of jerky, bouncing movements when you exercise. Such actions can stress joints and ligaments.

■ Make certain you warm up sufficiently. Try to do at least five minutes of muscle-warming exercises before beginning your exercise routine (see Chapter 7).

■ Cool down after exercising. To gradually lower your cardiovascular rate, try some easy walking, gentle stretching, or low-resistance stationary cycling after your workout.

■ Use caution when working out in hot, humid weather. Exercising when the temperature is high can lead to heat stress, which may include heat cramps when your muscles begin to spasm; heat exhaustion, when your heart rate increases and you feel dizzy, light-headed, weak, and/or nauseated; or even heat stroke, when the body is unable to dissipate heat. If you feel any of the symptoms of heat cramps or exhaustion starting, stop exercising and drink cool water. For heat stroke, get medical attention immediately.

■ Drink water. Forget the myth that drinking cold water while exercising will give you cramps, and drink plenty of water during your exercise period. Your body can't work at peak efficiency when deprived of adequate fluids, and serious dehydration can lead to a medical emergency.

■ If at all possible, learn to recognize whether you are exercising too strenuously by using your own rate of perceived exertion (see the Borg Scale, p. 67).

■ If you suffer from any chronic medical problems like asthma, hypertension, or arthritis, make sure you consult with your doctor before beginning any exercise program. Having a physical exam once a year will ensure that your health status has not changed.

4

NORMAL PREGNANCY
AND
FETAL DEVELOPMENT

The Pregnant Body

The body undergoes remarkable physiological changes in pregnancy, enabling the fetus to grow and preparing the woman for the delivery and nursing of the child. The processes that take place in the body of the expecting mother are primarily controlled by the hormone system and affect both the physical and emotional state of the woman.

27

■ *The Hormone System*

Pregnancy is a period of intense hormonal activity. Some hormones normally secreted by the body are produced in greater amounts, while others are released only during pregnancy. The pituitary—a small gland located in the center of the brain—increases in size two- or threefold, because its hormone-producing cells divide and become enlarged, and the hypothalamus (a part of the brain), the thyroid, and the pancreas also step up their hormone production. In addition, two new organs start releasing hormones: the corpus luteum and the placenta. The corpus luteum, formed in the ovaries during ovulation, usually disappears in the course of the menstrual cycle. When pregnancy occurs, however, it stays on and releases progesterone, human chorionic gonadotropin (hCG), estrogen, and other hormones. Since progesterone blocks the development of follicles—the ovarian structure that produces the ovum—the woman stops menstruating. The corpus luteum is active mostly during the first weeks of pregnancy, while the placenta takes over afterward. The hormone hCG, which appears only during pregnancy and is produced primarily in the first three months, is responsible for many unpleasant symptoms of pregnancy like excessive nausea. When its production subsides, the symptoms also disappear.

■ *The Nervous System*

Pregnancy affects transmission of signals throughout the nervous system and may therefore cause sleepiness, irritability, changes in appetite, taste, and smell, increased secretion of saliva, nausea, and sometimes vomiting.

■ *The Metabolism*

Normal metabolic processes are modified during pregnancy to suit the needs of the developing fetus. Oxygen consumption increases, as well as the protein content in body tissues. Carbohydrates accumulate in the liver, muscles, and the placenta; some fat deposits appear under the skin, particularly in the area of breasts and buttocks, and the concentration of certain types of fat and cholesterol in the blood increases. Salts of several minerals that are crucial for normal fetal development—including calcium, phosphorus, potassium, and iron—also accumulate in the pregnant body. Hormonal changes of pregnancy contribute to water retention in the tissues.

■ *The Cardiovascular System*

The workload of the cardiovascular system soars during pregnancy. New blood vessels form in the uterus, and a separate circulatory system develops in the placenta. Although its composition generally remains the same as before pregnancy, the volume of blood in the woman's circulation is close to double. In particular, blood supply to the uterus and the pelvic organs is increased. Under the strain, the heart has to pump harder, and its muscle is enlarged.

■ *The Respiratory System*

As the need for oxygen grows, the lungs must work harder to draw in more air. During pregnancy, breathing becomes somewhat deeper but not faster.

■ The External Genitalia and Uterus

The external genitals (vulva) often become enlarged and darken, and the mucous lining of the vagina grows bluish in color due to an increase in the number and size of blood vessels. The uterus grows larger, reaching its peak size by week 36: While before pregnancy it is approximately 3.5 inches long and 2.25 inches wide, at term its dimensions may reach 13.75 by 9 inches.

■ The Bones

Pregnancy hormones have a loosening effect on ligaments that provide support for many of the body's joints. In the pelvic area the laxity of joints serves to facilitate the birth of the baby. The bones of the pelvis become more mobile, and its width increases due to separation of bones of the pubis. The space gap between the pubic bones may reach up to ten millimeters.

■ The Skin

The effect of pregnancy on the skin is usually unpredictable. Skin that tended to be dry before pregnancy may become oily, and oily skin may grow dry. Sometimes, acne may clear up. Excessive dryness of the skin and itching, which are not uncommon during pregnancy, can be alleviated with body lotions, moisturizers, or talcum powder.

Many pregnant women develop stretch marks in those areas of the skin that are stretched out due to increased body size and hormonal changes.

In the third trimester many women develop dark patches on their skin. On the face, these patches are referred to as "pregnancy mask" or, in medical parlance, chloasma. Pigmented spots may also appear throughout the body, particularly at the midline. A dark streak called linea nigra may emerge below the navel toward the pubic bone. The pigmentation is due to increased production of the melanocyte-stimulating hormone by the pituitary gland. As its name suggests, this hormone stimulates the activity of melanin, the dark pigment that protects the skin against sunlight damage and is responsible for tanning.

The changes in skin pigmentation are temporary and will disappear after pregnancy. The woman should not try to erase the patches or streaks with bleaches or "scrubs." She can minimize the spots by avoiding the sun or using sunscreen and covering the spots that do appear with camouflage makeup.

▪ *The Breasts*

Under the influence of hormones and increased blood supply, breasts become engorged and firmer in pregnancy. During this time they are often tender and sensitive, but tenderness usually disappears by the middle months. A good maternity bra is likely to alleviate discomfort at least to some extent and may also help preserve the shape of the breasts after pregnancy is over.

Nipples become more prominent, and the areola around them changes color. It may become darker or, in fair-skinned women, more pink. Drops of secretion may already be squeezed from the nipples in the beginning of pregnancy, and several weeks before delivery a clear or milky discharge called colostrum appears. Although such leakage is normal in preparation for milk production, it can be bothersome. The woman, however, should not try to squeeze the colostrum out. Instead, she can wear breast pads or a soft tissue inside the bra to avoid discomfort.

■ *Weight Gain*

Due to the growth of the fetus, accumulation of amniotic fluid, buildup of interstitial body fluids and some fat deposits, enlargement of the uterus, and increase in the volume of blood, the woman steadily gains weight during pregnancy. The baby at birth weighs an average of 7.5 pounds and the uterus an average of 2.5 pounds—eighteen times its normal weight. Some four or five pounds are gained to provide a nutritional supply for the mother and fetus.

It was once believed that the pregnant woman should try not to gain much more than the probable weight of the baby. Now, however, physicians recommend that at least twenty-four pounds be gained during pregnancy to ensure proper development of the fetus. Women who are underweight should gain even more—up to thirty pounds— and women who are overweight should postpone weight-loss diets until pregnancy and nursing are over. After the third month a steady gain of approximately 0.75 pound per week is considered desirable. The caloric cost of pregnancy is approximately 300 calories a day, of nursing 500 calories a day.

■ *Pregnancy Sickness*

This is a very common complaint in pregnancy that affects about half of pregnant women in the first trimester. Although it is generally referred to as "morning sickness," episodes may in fact occur at any time of day. Sometimes they are accompanied by vomiting. The symptoms can be very disturbing for the woman, but they pose very little danger to the mother or the fetus.

It is not known what causes pregnancy sickness. Though it is thought that relaxation of the smooth muscle of the stomach may play a role, it is possible that high levels of hCG observed in the first trimester are also at fault. There is some evidence that symptoms are aggravated by emotional stress and by a diet high in protein and low in carbohydrates and vitamin B6. Changes in diet and mild exercise interspersed with rest can help minimize the illness. Sudden changes in position, such as the bending and stretching that are normally included in exercise routines, make these symptoms worse. They should be avoided and replaced by such activities as walking at a relaxed pace.

■ *The Weight of the Baby*

In the last three months of pregnancy the weight of the baby and its position in the uterus can cause discomfort to the woman. She experiences a frequent need to urinate because the growing uterus puts pressure on her bladder, and she cannot eat much at a time because of the pressure on her stomach. She may also find it more difficult to breathe, because her lung capacity is limited by the enlarging uterus and her diaphragm is displaced upward, sometimes by as much as one inch. To facilitate breathing, the woman may have to hold her back straight while sitting and standing, and sleep propped up with pillows or on her side. The vena cava, the vein that returns blood from the lower body to the heart, may also become compressed by the uterus. This leads to a drop in blood pressure in five to ten percent of pregnant women, precipitating nausea or a sensation of fainting. Particularly in the last trimester the woman should try to avoid lying on her back for more than a few minutes—the posture in which the vena cava is most likely to become compressed (see Fig. 3). In fact, if at all possible this

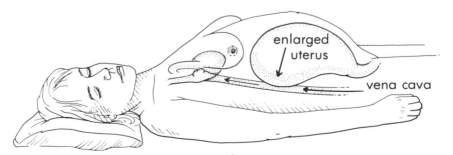

Fig. 3. Lying on your back during pregnancy places pressure on the vena cava, thereby reducing blood flow to the heart.

position should be avoided all through pregnancy, since many pregnant women will experience a lowering of their blood pressure whenever coming out of this supine position (lying on the back).

■ *Emotional Changes*

For both parents, pregnancy is a time of intense emotional responses, ranging from delight to anxiety. It is a period when anticipated pleasures of parenthood are mixed with worries and concerns about new responsibilities. The individual psychological makeup and changes taking place in the woman's body inevitably affect her mood. Since hormones exert a strong influence on the psyche, the woman's emotions are to some extent governed by modifications in her hormone system, which are very pronounced during pregnancy.

Vivid, disturbing dreams sometimes occur in pregnancy, indicating that the mind is preoccupied with concerns that are not always consciously expressed. Some women go through stages when they feel ambivalent or even negative about the pregnancy, which is quite normal and will have no effect on their ability to be good mothers. Negative emotions may be worsened by pregnancy sickness and fatigue. When these symptoms diminish by the second trimester, ambivalence often gives way to euphoria. Sudden swings of mood are very common, particularly during the first trimester, and are completely normal.

Fetal Development

The mean duration of pregnancy calculated from the first day of the last normal menstrual period is approximately 280 days or forty weeks, although some perfectly normal women may deliver one or two weeks earlier or later. Most women, however, ovulate and conceive some two weeks after their period, so when the pregnancy is said to be at ten weeks it is actually at eight weeks.

■ Fertilization and Implantation

Fertilization takes place in the fallopian tube when a male sperm merges with a female egg (ovum). Aided by the rhythmic contractions of the tube, the fertilized egg gradually moves toward the uterus—a journey that takes three or four days. During this time it divides into twelve to sixteen smaller cells that form a mulberrylike cluster no bigger in size than the original egg. In the uterus the cells begin to divide much faster, and by the end of the first week they invade the mucous lining of the uterus and implant themselves into its wall.

Hormonal changes characteristic of pregnancy start taking place in the woman's body from the moment of implantation. Sometimes, the fertilized egg may implant itself outside of the uterus, causing severe complications. When the implantation occurs in the cervix—the small, tight valve at the bottom of the uterus—it can cause severe bleeding and complications during delivery. Other sites of improper implantation leading to dangerous ectopic pregnancy include the fallopian tubes, the ovaries, and the abdominal cavity.

Although fetal development is one continuous process, it is customary to refer to the fertilized egg during the first three weeks as a blastocyst, from week 4 to week 8 as an embryo, and after week 8 as a fetus, the Latin for "offspring" (see Fig. 4).

■ Weeks 0 to 3—the Blastocyst

When the blastocyst implants in the lining of the uterus, it looks like a small, hollow sphere of cells. Its outer wall, called the trophoblast, has tiny fingerlike projections that pierce the uterine lining, anchoring the

Most of the internal organs are formed during the first trimester of pregnancy.

Second week:

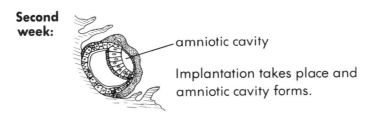

amniotic cavity

Implantation takes place and amniotic cavity forms.

Week 4:

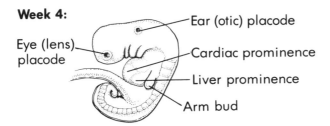

Ear (otic) placode

Eye (lens) placode

Cardiac prominence

Liver prominence

Arm bud

Weeks 4 to 8:

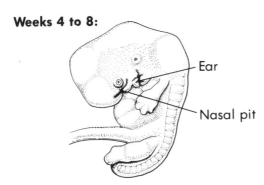

Ear

Nasal pit

End of week 12:

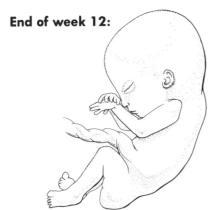

Limbs and internal organs are formed. Further growth and development occupy the two remaining trimesters.

Fig. 4.

blastocyst firmly in place. These fingers come in contact with the woman's blood vessels, establishing the first link between embryo and mother. The trophoblast gradually thickens and becomes a fully functioning placenta—a circular, fleshlike tissue through which the mother's blood, nutrients, and oxygen nourish the fetus.

During the second week a small, thin-walled space called the amniotic cavity appears in the blastocyst. In later weeks it will expand and fill up with amniotic fluid, accommodating the whole baby.

By the third week the rapidly dividing cells of the blastocyst group into three layers. The grouping is the beginning of differentiation, a process in the course of which cells are assigned their unique future function. Cells of the lower layer, the endoderm, will create internal organs of the body—the digestive tract, the liver, and the lungs. The middle layer, the mesoderm, will develop into the muscles and blood. The upper layer, the ectoderm, will give rise to the skin, hair, nails, and the nervous system.

The three layers are present in all animals and give rise to the same type of organ in each species. For example, the ectoderm, which develops into skin in humans, forms the scales in fish and the feathers in birds.

With differentiation, the blastocyst changes from a disklike mass into an embryonic form that has a distinct head and tail. Such essential organs as the brain and the heart begin to form at this stage, as well as a primitive circulatory system. The heart will undergo numerous changes before it becomes the complicated four-chambered muscular pump that beats in the chest of human beings, but even at this rudimentary stage it starts to contract and pump the blood through the embryo and the placenta.

By the beginning of the fourth week the embryo is suspended on a body stalk through which it receives nutrients. The stalk will later develop into the umbilical cord, connecting the embryo with the placenta.

■ *Weeks 4 to 8—the Embryonic Period*

Weeks 4 to 8 are a critical period of fetal development because many crucial organs start forming at this time and the nervous system and blood circulation undergo dramatic changes. Although at week 4 the embryo is only a quarter inch long, almost all the organs have begun to form. During this period the embryo is particularly vulnerable to external factors that can cause birth defects, such as exposure to drugs or radiation. It is during this stage that hyperthermia (high body core temperature) generated by strenuous exercise could potentially affect the development of the nervous system.

The gallbladder, stomach, and certain areas of the brain begin to form during week 4, as well as the thyroid, larynx, and trachea. The heartbeat grows sufficiently strong to be visualized by ultrasound. By week 5, arms and legs form distinguishable limb buds, and the liver and kidneys begin to develop. Parts of the head—nose, mouth, eyes, ears, and regional divisions of the brain—also appear in week 5. At this stage the eyes are located on either side of the head, and gill slits appear behind each eye, a leftover from the evolutionary process.

By the end of week 6, the embryo is about one inch long and has a recognizable human appearance. Its head is proportionately very large, comprising one-third of the body length. Its heart has finished forming and has four chambers. It is at this stage that congenital heart defects may appear due to improper fusing of the heart parts.

By the end of week 8 the embryo's tail has disappeared and centers of bone growth have been established. The nose and upper jaw develop rapidly, the two sides of the lips and palate fuse, and tooth buds appear. After this stage is complete, such defects as harelip and cleft palate cannot occur.

■ The Third Month—Weeks 9 to 12

At the beginning of the ninth week the baby, which is now called a fetus, is about 1.5 inches long. Its eyes have moved to the front of the head, and the ears, which originated in the neck, have moved to the sides of the head. A cartilage model of the skeleton is formed, later to be replaced by true calcified bone. Movements of the arms and legs can be detected by ultrasound, although the mother cannot yet feel them.

The fetus continues to grow rapidly until about week 20, when the rate of its increase in length slows down. By the end of the twelfth week the formation of its limbs and internal organs is completed, and the risk of major structural abnormality occurring at a later stage in pregnancy is very small. The external genitalia are now quite developed, and the sex of the fetus can be discerned on ultrasound. The amniotic sac has expanded and contains about twelve ounces of fluid. Amniotic fluid swallowed by the fetus is involved in its development and growth.

The fetus maintains its own circulatory system, although its lungs are not equipped to oxygenate the blood. Instead, fetal blood is oxygenated in the placenta, and carbon dioxide and waste products are extracted through the umbilical cord to the placenta and the mother's body.

The placenta performs four crucial tasks: It filters oxygen and nourishment from the mother's blood via the umbilical cord, removes carbon dioxide and waste products from the fetus, blocks the transmission of some, albeit not all, infections and drugs, and produces hormones vital for the normal development of the pregnancy.

■ The Fourth Month—Weeks 13 to 16

Developments that occur in the first three months are much more dramatic than any changes taking place in the remainder of pregnancy. From now on, the organs that formed in the early weeks grow larger and mature. The skin of the fetus becomes thicker, although it is still red. The fetus looks like a baby, with fully developed arms, legs, and head, and fully separated fingers and toes. The proportion of different body parts, however, will still undergo some changes—the legs will become longer and the head relatively smaller. The head is quite round, and the bulge of the forebrain can be distinguished from the cerebellum and brain stem. Since three-quarters of miscarriages—spontaneous abortions—occur in the first trimester, by the fourth month the risk of miscarriage is much lower. The fetus, however, is way too under-developed to survive outside the womb.

■ *The Fifth Month—Weeks 17 to 20*

The fetus is still growing rapidly, and by the middle of the fifth month weighs about twelve ounces. It is about ten inches long, although the precise length is difficult to judge because its spine began to curve at the end of the third month. The amniotic sac is now so large that the fetus can move about and rotate, and it is now that the mother will feel the baby kick for the first time. The kicks grow more vigorous as the pregnancy progresses, although some babies are more active than others. The fetus has alternating periods of rest and activity that may be influenced by the sleep/wake cycle of the mother.

Thin, downy hair called lanugo begins to grow on the eyebrows and upper lip of the fetus and toward the end of the fifth month covers its entire body. Before birth the hair is shed from all parts of the body except the eyelashes, eyebrows, and scalp. Some babies, much to the bewilderment of their mothers, are born while still covered with lanugo, which is shed shortly afterward. It is not known whether lanugo serves a purpose or whether it is nothing but a leftover from species evolution. At a later stage it is replaced by hair growing from secondary follicles.

The body of the fetus also starts covering up with vernix caseosa, a creamy white substance secreted by oil glands in its skin. Vernix caseosa, which protects the skin from the dampness of the amniotic fluid, first appears on the back, in the hair, and in joint creases, and eventually covers the whole body.

▪ The Sixth Month—Weeks 21 to 24

At the beginning of this month the ovaries or testicles are structurally established, the tubules of the kidneys branch out, and the bronchial tube continues to branch. Skin ridges develop on the palms of the hands and the soles of the feet. Eyebrows and eyelashes are evident.

The last months of fetal development are an important period of growth for the brain. The developing brain cells require nourishment, and while the mother is advised to eat a balanced diet rich in vitamins and other nutrients throughout pregnancy, good, balanced nutrition is particularly crucial in the last four or five months of pregnancy.

▪ The Seventh Month—Weeks 25 to 28

The fetus now has longer hair, eyelashes, and eyebrows, and can open and close its eyes. The pigment that determines eye color develops in the iris after birth, which is why the eyes of all newborn babies are pale blue.

The lanugo begins to disappear, and the skin changes color from red to pink due to deposits of fat that build up under the skin. In boys, the testicles, which form in the abdomen, begin to descend to the scrotum.

All the vital organs have been formed, and from the end of the seventh month until delivery the fetus primarily grows in weight and size. Babies born at this stage have up to a seventy-five percent chance of survival, although they often require intensive medical care. Larger babies may grow up completely normal, but the ones that are very premature may suffer from serious neurological and other disorders.

■ *The Eighth Month—Weeks 29 to 32*

By the middle of this month the fetus weighs about 3.5 pounds, the placenta about one pound, and there are about three pints of amniotic fluid. The fetus still looks rather thin, although more fat has been deposited under its skin. Its lungs and other organs are still immature, and the skull is not fully ossified, but babies born at this time have a good chance of survival if placed immediately in a premature-baby unit.

The fetal heart beats very fast, at about twice the rate of the mother's pulse, and it can be easily heard with a stethoscope. The baby's position by now is probably head down, toward the mother's pelvis.

■ *The Ninth Month—Weeks 33 to 36*

At the middle of the ninth month the baby's appearance is the same as it will be at birth—the head is in better proportion to the body, and the skin is less wrinkled because more fat has built up underneath the skin. Because the fetus is now larger—it weighs approximately 5.5 pounds and is seventeen to eighteen inches long—it cannot rotate freely in the uterus. The mother may feel very uncomfortable because the baby is pressing on her lungs and stomach until it moves down into the pelvis in preparation for birth. At term, the baby will weigh on average 7.5 pounds, but some normal, healthy babies weigh less and others weigh more.

The duration of normal pregnancies varies. Some fetuses mature and grow in size faster than others, which may have an effect on the onset of labor. Twins, for example, are often born prematurely, because their combined weight may speed up the approach of labor. In addition, the estimated due date often turns out to be incorrect because the precise moment of conception is usually unknown, and many babies are born three weeks before or one and one-half weeks after the expected timing. If, however, labor has not begun at one and one-half to two weeks past the expected date, the baby must be monitored closely to ensure it is not deprived of nutrients and oxygen as the placenta begins to age. If the baby is well, the mother may be advised to wait until labor begins spontaneously, although in some instances it may be necessary to induce labor or perform a cesarean section if the baby's size is excessive.

5

PHYSIOLOGICAL EFFECTS OF EXERCISE ON THE PREGNANT BODY AND FETUS

Exercise provokes rapid changes in body chemistry that require a variety of physiological adjustments. In many ways, the body perceives exercise, particularly when it is strenuous, as a form of stress: Additional fuel resources are mobilized, the heart rate and level of perspiration increase, alertness becomes more acute.

The effects of exercise on the human body have been extensively studied. Some of these are familiar to all, such as the effects on the heart and breathing. The workload of the heart, for example, may increase eightfold during vigorous exercise. In fact, heart rate has been the most popular method for prescribing individual training programs tailored to the person's age, sex, and physical fitness. Less well known are the effects of exercise on metabolism, hormone levels, temperature control, and fluid balance, although these aspects are also taken into account when training schedules are designed. Some health conditions, such as diabetes or heart disease, require particular caution in the design of exercise programs.

Exercise programs for pregnant women need to take into account the physiological changes that normally occur in pregnancy, such as increases in the heart rate, blood volume, and fetal needs. Moreover, special attention must be given to the specific effects of exercise on the pregnant as opposed to nonpregnant body.

Until recently, little was known about the way physical exertion affects different organs and body systems in pregnancy. The dearth of data often leads to a cautious approach discouraging pregnant women from undertaking any exercise at all. However, studies on exercise physiology during pregnancy conducted in the past few years have for the first time provided a scientific basis for advising women on the level of activity they can maintain while pregnant without jeopardizing their health or that of their unborn babies.

New findings have shown that recommendations about exercise in pregnancy should best be made on an individual basis for each woman. Thus, while most pregnant women can probably benefit from exercise, others should avoid it to prevent damage to their own well-being and that of their fetus.

The Pregnant Body

■ The Hormone System

Since changes in the pregnant body are largely governed by hormones, pregnancy is a time of numerous hormonal upheavals. During exercise, these are combined with hormonal changes triggered by physical activity. The hormone system to a great extent determines all other adjustments to exercise that occur in the body, such as the response of the respiratory and cardiovascular systems.

In a healthy pregnant woman, hormonal changes induced by exercise are transient and reversible and appear to cause no damage to the fetus. Overall, the level of all hormones rises in the course of exercise both in pregnant and nonpregnant individuals, although the rate of the increase may vary.

The response depends greatly on the type, intensity, and duration of exercise. When produced by mild and moderate exercise it lasts approximately fifteen minutes, after which hormone levels in the pregnant woman return to their previous values. Strenuous physical activity provokes longer-lasting changes that can persist for thirty minutes or more.

The hormonal response can be diminished with training. For example, levels of some stress hormones fail to rise as sharply after a certain period of exercise conditioning.

EPINEPHRINE

Epinephrine, or adrenaline, is the first hormone to respond to stress. It mobilizes energy resources and regulates the action of other hormones in stressful situations, including exercise. During mild and moderate exercise the rise in epinephrine levels is minimal and not threatening to the mother and fetus.

However, with strenuous exercise the rise in epinephrine is less pronounced in pregnant as compared with nonpregnant women, suggesting a possible protection mechanism for the vital energy supply to the fetus.

NOREPINEPHRINE

Norepinephrine, or noradrenaline as it is referred to in common usage, is a stress hormone that stimulates muscle fibers and causes muscles to contract. Its rise during exercise is particularly pronounced in pregnancy.

In a normal, healthy pregnancy the rise in norepinephrine poses no danger. Potential risk may arise in women who are at risk of premature labor, because a significant increase in the levels of the hormone can stimulate the uterus to contract excessively.

CORTISOL

Cortisol has a mechanism of action similar to that of adrenaline, but its response to stress is more delayed. Its effects are also different, including increase in blood sugar levels and fluid retention. Concentration of cortisol in the blood rises steadily during pregnancy. Theoretically, the increase should enhance exercise performance and endurance of the pregnant woman, but there is no evidence for such an effect, probably due to a very limited role of this hormone in the physiology of exercise. In pregnancy, exercise produces only insignificant changes in cortisol levels.

OPIOIDS

Levels of opioid hormones—beta-endorphin and beta-lipotropin—double or even triple during vigorous exercise. Since these hormones have a natural pain-killing effect, they may blunt the perception of labor pain. According to some reports, women who are physically fit and exercise during pregnancy tend to have less painful labor, which may be a result of a higher concentration of opioids in their bodies.

■ *The Cardiovascular System*

During pregnancy the cardiovascular system of the woman undergoes significant changes: The blood volume and heart rate increase, as does the amount of blood pumped through the heart with each beat, while arterial blood pressure decreases. More blood is channeled to internal organs and less to muscles. Thus, the uterus of a pregnant woman receives 500 ml more blood per minute than that of a nonpregnant woman. These changes are part of normal adjustments to pregnancy and must also be taken into account when an exercise program for a pregnant woman is prescribed.

In healthy nonpregnant subjects, exercise prescription is often based on the so-called target heart rate, which is calculated on the basis of the maximal rate the heart can reach. Depending on the person's age, sex, and fitness, the target value can constitute sixty to ninety percent of the maximal heart rate. People are considered physically fit if they can engage in intensive exercise at the target heart rate and maintain this level of activity for a certain period of time.

In pregnant women the relationship between the heart rate and the growing requirements of the body during exercise is complicated by the changes associated with pregnancy. With mild and moderate exercise the heart rate slightly increases, as does the amount of blood pumped with each beat. If, however, the intensity of the exercise continues to increase, the rise in the heart rate starts to lag behind. With strenuous exercise, the maximal heart rate the pregnant woman can reach is lower than the value she would have achieved if she were not pregnant. Thus, exercise prescription in pregnancy cannot be based on heart rate alone.

■ *Blood Flow*

During exercise more blood flows to the working muscles and less to internal organs, including the uterus. The redistribution can potentially restrict oxygen supply to the fetus. However, to affect fetal oxygen supply the flow of blood to the uterus must be reduced by more than fifty percent. Such a reduction is highly unlikely to occur in a normal healthy pregnant woman during mild or moderate exercise, but could take place when exercise is strenuous and prolonged.

The flow of blood through the placenta could be further reduced by the rise in the mother's stress hormones that occurs with exercise, because two of these hormones—epinephrine and norepinephrine—have the effect of constricting blood vessels. However, the placenta disposes of these substances very efficiently, and under normal conditions only ten to fifteen percent of norepinephrine and epinephrine in the mother's circulation reaches the fetus.

▪ Energy Resources

Use of energy resources in pregnancy is governed by the constant need to provide an adequate supply of nutrients to the fetus. All available resources—fats, proteins, and carbohydrates—are mobilized to channel energy to the fetus without harming the mother.

The effect of exercise on fuel supply is somewhat different in pregnant as opposed to nonpregnant individuals. Usually, mild to moderate exercise has very little effect on sugar levels in the blood, and most of the energy comes from fat. When exercise is strenuous or prolonged, carbohydrates become the primary source of energy. In pregnancy, however, blood sugar is the predominant source of fuel during exercise, particularly with great or lasting physical exertion. A steady supply of carbohydrates comes from the liver, which stores glucose in a form called glycogen.

A pregnant woman engaging in prolonged exercise runs the risk of depleting fuel resources, with potential significant side effects to the fetus. Prolonged exercise can sometimes lead to hypoglycemia, deficiency of sugar in the blood—a highly undesirable condition during pregnancy that may cause birth defects or even fetal death. There are known anecdotes, but not scientific reports. The risk of exercise-associated hypoglycemia appears to be higher during pregnancy.

▪ Breathing

Anatomical changes that occur during pregnancy put a strain on the woman's respiratory system. Her nose, throat, and other passages in the upper respiratory tract may be swollen or obstructed by excessive secretions. Her rib cage expands forward, but its volume is restricted from below by the increasing size of the uterus, particularly during the second half of pregnancy. At the same time, her need for oxygen grows and its consumption increases by ten to twenty percent.

The pregnant woman ensures an adequate supply of oxygen for herself and her fetus by breathing deeper. When she exerts no physical effort, she breathes in more than sufficient amounts of air and oxygen. Exercise, however, adds extra strain on the respiratory system, while the lungs have only a limited space to expand and accommodate more air. As a result, oxygen reserves available to an exercising pregnant woman are limited and reduced compared with nonpregnant individuals.

The mechanism of oxygen consumption also plays an important role in understanding the effects of exercise on the pregnant body. During the initial stage of exercise, the heart and respiratory system are not capable of providing sufficient amounts of oxygen rapidly. As a result, muscles borrow oxygen from their energy reserves. During the recovery period after exercise, the muscle returns the "debt" by extracting more oxygen from the blood. In pregnancy, too high a deficit in oxygen is undesirable because it may affect the fetus.

As the pregnancy progresses, amounts of oxygen required to perform the same type of exercise increase. This is particularly true for weight-dependent exercise—activities in which the weight of the woman plays a role, such as walking or jogging. In contrast, in such activities as swimming or bicycle riding, for example, energy and oxygen demands are not dependent on the woman's weight. Because the heart of a pregnant woman has a limited capacity to keep up with the increasing demand for oxygen, intensity of weight-dependent exercise may have to be decreased as pregnancy progresses.

■ *Body Temperature*

As we exercise, our body temperature goes up because we are burning energy resources to get the fuel for the vigorous activity. This increase must be taken into account as pregnant women exercise, because the mother's heat can be transferred across the placenta to the fetus. Since the fetus cannot sweat and has no other mechanism for getting rid of excess heat, it can lead to possible birth defects. Studies have shown that offspring of research animals that were exposed in early gestation to temperatures above 39 degrees C (102.2 degrees F) had a high incidence of congenital malformations like spina bifida, a defect of the spine that can lead to paralysis of the lower part of the body.

It has not yet been confirmed whether human babies are similarly threatened by exposure to heat, but women are advised to avoid overheating in the first trimester of pregnancy when most vital organs and body parts of the fetus are formed.

■ Pregnancy Outcomes

Several studies have recently sought to investigate the possible connection between exercise in pregnancy and such complications as spontaneous abortion, uterine bleeding, premature labor, and others. Researchers have also looked into the effect of exercise on duration of labor, postpartum recovery, and other aspects of pregnancy outcome.

At present, no study has shown whether exercise is harmful or beneficial for pregnancy outcome. The problem with all the studies, however, is that they involved only a small number of women and mostly those who were quite athletic prior to pregnancy.

The Fetus

■ *The Heart*

Fetal heart rate is the most accessible indicator of the well-being of the fetus. It provides the obstetrician with the means of detecting such threatening conditions as lack of oxygen supply, suffocation, or fetal distress. Deprived of enough oxygen, for example, the fetal heart slows down.

Measuring fetal heart rate during exercise is technically very difficult. Fetal-monitoring equipment is designed to be used when the woman is not moving. It emits ultrasound waves that penetrate the abdomen and bounce off the fluids and tissues in the uterus. The reflected waves are translated into an electrical signal that provides information about the vital signs of the fetus. The woman's movements can disturb the signal or drown the heart rate of the fetus. However, in some cases it is possible to record fetal heartbeat while the mother is exercising, and such recordings have been done.

Recently, in an experiment conducted by one of the authors of this book, fetal heart rate was for the first time recorded during maternal exercise in labor. The monitoring in this case could be performed with great accuracy, because in labor the amniotic sac harboring the fetus could be ruptured and electrodes could be attached directly to the scalp of the fetus. The two mothers who participated in the experiment were both elite athletes. They rode a stationary bicycle while in labor, with electrodes of the monitoring device attached to the head of the fetus. It was found that fetal heart rate did not change throughout the three and one-half minutes that the exercise lasted.

INCREASE IN THE FETAL HEART RATE

By and large, the fetus responds to maternal exercise by an increase in the heart rate of ten to thirty beats per minute. The heartbeat remains elevated for about five minutes, then declines and goes back to its previous value within fifteen minutes.

SLOWING OF THE FETAL HEART RATE

Slowing down can signal fetal distress, due to cord compression or placental insufficiency. However, maternal exercise occasionally leads to a slowing down in the heartbeat of the fetus that appears to be transient and harmless. When the mother has rested after the exercise, the fetal heartbeat picks up and even accelerates for a short while, apparently in compensation.

When the slowing down was first observed, it was attributed to insufficient oxygen supply due to the decrease of blood flow to the uterus. However, under normal conditions oxygen reserves in the uterus largely exceed the needs of the fetus. The mother must lose thirty percent of her blood for the fetal heart rate to slow down. Therefore, the slowing down probably occurs as a reflex to changes precipitated by hormones that rise during maternal exercise.

■ *Oxygen Supply*

The fetus requires a virtually continuous supply of oxygen and nutrients to maintain normal growth and development. The amount of oxygen delivered to the fetus through the placenta depends on the flow of maternal and fetal blood, concentrations of hemoglobin in the blood, and the levels of oxygen in the arteries. Some of these factors are affected by exercise. Thus, the flow of blood to the uterus drops, decreasing oxygen supply.

Faced with a decrease in oxygen transfer, the fetus responds with a number of mechanisms that can temporarily protect it against this dangerous and potentially fatal condition. One of these is redistribution of blood: More blood starts to flow to such vital organs as the heart, brain, and adrenal gland, and less to organs less crucial for survival, like the liver, spleen, gut, and kidney. This mechanism, however, appears to have its limits. Animal experiments have shown that when blood flow to the uterus drops by fifty percent for ten minutes, redistribution ensures adequate oxygen consumption by the vital organs. If, however, normal blood flow is reduced by seventy-five percent, the pregnant body is no longer able to compensate the heart and the brain of the fetus for the decrease in oxygen supply.

■ Fetal Movements

Activity in the womb reflects the well-being of the developing fetus. On average, the fetus moves three to twelve minutes every hour. Toward the end of pregnancy the fetus also makes movements to breathe. While there is no air in the amniotic sac, these motions are a leftover of an evolutionary process and probably help develop a primitive breathing reflex in the baby. Breathing movements occur sporadically about one-third of the time during the last trimester.

Movements appears to be a good indicator of how the fetus is doing not only throughout the whole pregnancy but during exercise as well. While the woman is engaged in exercise and immediately afterward, the fetus generally starts moving more. Fetuses of mothers with high blood pressure tend to move less following exercise and are suspected of being distressed.

■ Weight of the Fetus

Most effects of maternal exercise on the fetus appear to be transitory, but strenuous exercise may have some undesirable and lasting consequences, notably reduction in the weight of the fetus. Infants of working mothers, for example, weigh as much as four hundred grams (approximately 1 pound) less than average at birth. According to a recent study, women who engage in strenuous exercise before and during pregnancy gain less weight, deliver eight days earlier than normally expected, and have infants with birth weights five hundred grams less than average. The cause of reduced birth weight and growth retardation in the womb is probably due to reduced fuel transfer across the placenta. These findings appear to warrant caution with respect to strenuous physical activity during pregnancy.

Pregnant Diabetic Patients

Some of the pregnancy hormones tend to block the action of insulin, the protein responsible for sugar metabolism that is lacking in diabetics. Thus pregnancy, which is characterized by a sharp rise in hormone levels, can sometimes trigger a condition similar to diabetes. It is most likely to occur in women prone to hyperglycemia (excess of sugar in the blood) and intolerance to glucose. These disorders can cause difficulty in pregnancy and in delivery, causing a higher incidence of problems like macrosomia (large babies), low blood sugar, respiratory distress, and jaundice in the fetus. Diabetic patients, in turn, often experience a worsening of their condition during pregnancy.

Exercise has long been used to normalize blood sugar levels in adult-onset diabetes. Paradoxically, it may increase blood sugar in juvenile diabetics who have no insulin and depend on outside administration of insulin.

Pregnant diabetic women have been traditionally denied the option of exercising, primarily due to the fear of causing damage to the fetus. Recent studies, however, have shown that mild to moderate exercise appears to have no adverse effect on the outcome of pregnancy in patients with adult-onset diabetes. In fact, exercise is beneficial for these women, as it may allow them to forgo medication and rely on their own insulin instead. However, pregnant diabetic patients should exercise only under medical supervision.

6

GENERAL GUIDELINES FOR EXERCISE DURING PREGNANCY

When today's active women become pregnant they're eager to continue the exercise and sports activities they enjoyed prior to pregnancy. And for the most part there's no reason why they shouldn't. Studies at our laboratory and others around the country involving hundreds of women demonstrate that *moderate* aerobic exercise and sports participation during pregnancy may offer many health benefits.

Statistical studies show that more than ninety-nine percent of the people who exercise do so to derive health benefits and that less than one percent are athletes or others who do so to improve performance. Thus, exercise guidelines in this book are directed to the majority of exercising women whose goal is to derive health benefits. Elite athletes may find these guidelines overly restrictive and may require an individualized, medically supervised exercise regimen to maintain their performance level.

The health benefits of regular exercise include:

- A more comfortable pregnancy.
- Maintenance of cardiovascular and respiratory fitness.
- Possible prevention of varicose veins, leg cramps, and thrombosis (blood clotting).
- Promotion of muscle tone and strength.
- Improved control of balance and coordination.
- Increased energy levels.
- A more positive emotional outlook and enhanced feelings of well-being.
- An easier and quicker return to prepregnancy weight and fitness.

It is important, however, to approach the issue of exercise during pregnancy with objectivity. As emphasized throughout this book, we believe that pregnancy should not be a state of confinement. Although we accept the premise that a certain amount of regular physical activity increases physical fitness and enhances our sense of well-being, there is no proof that it benefits the outcome of pregnancy. Nor is there scientific proof that a sedentary life-style is necessarily detrimental.

In addition, there is a downside for pregnant women who engage in overly strenuous exercise or the wrong kind of physical activity. For one thing, the mother's need for oxygen increases as exercise intensifies, so during a strenuous workout adequate blood and oxygen may not be delivered to the fetus. Of course, oxygen is not the only vital nutrient carried in the bloodstream. When rigorous exercise shunts blood away from the uterus toward the mother's working muscles, the fetus may be deprived not only of necessary oxygen but of other nutrients as well. In the extreme, this can cause fetal distress. Studies suggest that while the heart rate of the fetus actually does not change or increases after the mother exercises, during the workout period the fetal heart rate may occasionally drop. If exercise is too rigorous, bradycardia (the abnormally slow beating of the heart) may occur, which could lead to periods of fetal asphyxia (too little oxygen while excessive carbon dioxide accumulates) and consequent fetal distress.

The extra weight carried during pregnancy makes exercise harder work. Your heart rate during pregnancy is higher than usual even when resting, and it increases more quickly when you work out and must be monitored, particularly during prolonged and rigorous exercise, to ensure that you are not placing your own health at risk and overtaxing your heart.

Strenuous exercise during pregnancy may also lead to a potentially dangerous condition called hyperthermia, which is an excessively high body temperature (in excess of 101 degrees F or 38 degrees C). Normally, the fetus dissipates its own excess heat across the placenta through the bloodstream in a process similar to the way you dissipate your own excess heat through your skin. (Remember, though, the fetus has no other mechanisms like perspiration or respiration to cool itself off.) But if the mother's body temperature becomes excessively high, then the transfer of heat from the fetus to the mother may be reversed, producing a rise in fetal temperature and increasing the chances of organ damage, miscarriage, and fetal distress.

■ *General Guidelines*

It is the preceding potential risks to mothers and their fetuses that make exercise guidelines for pregnant women so important. The usual recommendations for nonpregnant women (namely, that it's okay to begin an exercise regimen without consulting a physician if you are under thirty-five, have no evidence or history of cardiovascular disease, are not at risk for coronary disease, and have had a medical evaluation during the previous year) fail to address the special needs of a pregnant woman. In most cases these women simply have been told not to "overdo" it and to rely on common sense when participating in any exercise program.

Yet since today's pregnant women are involved in such a wide range of physical activities, we believe they need to understand both the general and specific do's and don'ts of exercise, and sports, and pregnancy. Thus, our guidelines are in keeping with those of the American College of Obstetricians and Gynecologists (see Table 6:1). In addition, we offer the following broad-stroke guidelines for exercise during pregnancy.

■ Once you learn that you are pregnant, consult a physician about the kinds of physical exercise in which you can healthfully and safely engage. With a few exceptions, you should be able to continue your prepregnancy exercise regimen with some modification of the level of rigorousness. Although we don't recommend taking up any new and strenuous activity during pregnancy, particularly if you have been fairly sedentary before, you can begin a low-intensity exercise program. Pregnancy is a time of increased body awareness, and certainly behavior modification could result in habits that will benefit you and your family for the rest of your life. Again, however, be sure to check with your physician before initiating any exercise regimen.

■ Understand your medical history and any special health risks associated with it. Most likely, your doctor will advise you to restrict your activities if you have a history of heart disease, high blood pressure, spontaneous abortions or premature labor, an incompetent cervix, placenta previa (a condition in which the placenta lies across the opening of the uterus), or vaginal bleeding. You also may have to limit your activity level if you have juvenile diabetes, thyroid disease, anemia or other blood disorders, or if you are excessively over- or under-weight.

■ Begin each exercise period, including a sports activity, with a ten- to fifteen-minute warm-up period. This is necessary to prevent injury, balance the muscle development, and prepare the cardiovascular system for the stress of exercise. Effective warm-up exercises include slow, large movements such as arm circling, slow walking, or stationary cycling at low resistance and gentle stretching exercises of the neck, shoulder, trunk, hip, calf, and hamstring.

■ End each workout with ten- to fifteen-minute cool-down session that emphasizes walking around for a few minutes until your breathing and heart rate have gone down to normal. Then repeat the same gentle muscle stretching that you used to begin your exercise session.

Avoid excessive stretching, however, which can strain ligaments that are already loosened by the hormonal changes of pregnancy.

■ Never exercise when the temperature and/or humidity is high or when you have any fever. Under these conditions, exercise may

---

Table 6:1 Guidelines of the American College of Obstetricians and Gynecologists (ACOG) for Exercise During Pregnancy

---

The following are excerpted from the exercise guidelines issued by ACOG in 1992:

1. Any exercise program must be safe and enjoyable.
2. When uncertain, err on the side of safety.
3. Exercise programs for pregnant women can benefit them by promoting strength and coordination.
4. Regular exercise is preferable to occasional workouts. Exercise should be undertaken 3 to 5 days a week.
5. Pregnant women are advised not to exceed a heart rate of 140 beats per minute while exercising in an unsupervised environment. The rate of perceived exertion should not exceed RPE-14 (somewhat hard). See page 67.
6. To prevent musculoskeletal injuries, warm-ups and cool-downs are recommended. The progressive laxity of joints and ligaments predisposes pregnant women to injuries. This is also the rationale for recommending against excessive stretching in pregnancy.
7. Pregnant women should be advised that the strenuous portion of their exercise routine should not exceed fifteen to twenty minutes. This is precautionary advice to prevent increased body temperature (hyperthermia) and musculoskeletal injuries. Lower intensity aerobic activities may be conducted for as long as forty-five minutes.
8. Proper caloric and fluid intake are essential.
9. Resistance training: lifting weights against resistance promotes muscle toning, and one set of such exercises may be conducted at least twice a week, with a period of at least 24 hours between each session. Light weights (1 to 3 kg, 2 to 5 pounds) should be used to prevent injuries to joints and ligaments.
10. To avoid potential risks, pregnant women should avoid the following:

■ Exercise in the supine position.
■ Exercise that involves straining (the Valsalva maneuver).
■ Rise in body core temperature, which should not exceed 38 degrees C or 100.4 degrees F.
■ Jerky (ballistic) movements.

further raise your body's core temperature, resulting in hyperthermia and its potentially harmful consequences.

■ Never exercise to the point of exhaustion. Again, hyperthermia might occur and put you and your fetus at risk; it may also precipitate premature labor.

■ Drink plenty of water before and during exercise to prevent dehydration.

■ Wear appropriate clothing to permit free evaporation of sweat and cool the body down.

■ Exercise regularly, at least three times a week. Less frequent or intermittent exercise can overstress the body.

■ Don't use a sauna or hot tub during pregnancy. Many exercise clubs and other facilities have saunas or hot tubs for use after exercise. These should be avoided during pregnancy because they can raise internal body temperature and harm the fetus. (If, however, you are accustomed to using a sauna or hot tub and do not want to be deprived of it during pregnancy, limit your time in it to less than ten minutes.)

■ Undergo periodic testing by your physician to assess the effect of your exercise program on the fetus and make any necessary adjustments.

■ *Before Beginning an Exercise Program*

As stressed earlier, before entering an exercise program it is essential that you see your obstetrician or primary-care physician for a physical examination. This is needed to ensure that both you and your baby are well and that your exercise activities will not harm either of you. *Although physical activities entail theoretical risks, as outlined in earlier chapters, the likelihood of harm to you and your baby is remote provided you are healthy and your pregnancy is uncomplicated.*

Unless you are training for a major competitive event such as the Olympics while planning your pregnancy exercise program, and since you don't want to take any risk of harm to yourself or your baby, *moderation* is the key word. Reducing your prepregnancy exercise by one-third should achieve this objective. In advising their pregnant patients about exercise, obstetricians generally refer to the guidelines listed in Table 6:1. In addition, it is essential that you:

1. Know the risks.
2. Know your physical abilities and limitations.

Increased awareness on your part of the potential risks will minimize your chances of injury. Furthermore, you need to realistically recognize your physical fitness abilities. While physical fitness is not a requirement for a healthy pregnancy, many women insist that fitness makes life at this time more enjoyable, and in the long run fitness provides benefits in terms of health and well-being. If you were sedentary prior to pregnancy, you need not be discouraged from engaging in physical activities. However, you may want to be extra cautious to avoid injuries.

In addition to assessing your fitness level, you should also know how to use what is referred to as the RPE Scale, which is a rating of perceived exertion (see Table 6:4). The scale, which was developed by a Swedish physiologist named Borg (no relation to the tennis player), allows exercisers to correlate their perceived activity level with total exertion and aerobic capacity. Although the Borg Scale is not as accurate as laboratory testing, it provides a method to estimate total exertion and physical fatigue. Try to estimate your feelings of exertion as accurately as possible, without over- or underestimation.

Regardless of your fitness level, we recommend that during pregnancy, you exercise at a perceived level no higher than *moderate to somewhat strong*, or 12 to 14 on the RPE Scale. From time to time you should refer to the RPE Scale to make sure that you are still within these limits. Numerous factors alter your fitness level, especially during pregnancy. For example, a week or so of inactivity because of bad weather, a cold, or some other intervening factor may result in a significant drop in your level of fitness.

Table 6:2 CALCULATING THE TRAINING HEART RATE (THR)

The following formula may be used to calculate the training heart rate (THR) for most persons who are not pregnant.

Estimate:

220 − age = Maximum Heart Rate (MHR) × 60 to 70 percent

To obtain the training heart rate, multiply the maximum heart rate by 60 to 70 percent, depending upon the desired intensity of training.

Example: For a 35-year-old nonpregnant woman who wishes to train at a moderate 65 percent of intensity, her training heart rate is:

220 − 35 = MHR, 175 beats per minute

65 percent of 175 = 134

A more complicated formula involving the resting heart rate (the number of heartbeats per minute when a person is resting) is:

(220 − age) − Resting Heart Rate × 60 percent + Resting Heart Rate = THR

Example: For a 35-year-old woman who has a resting heart rate of 70 and is training at 60 percent of intensity, her training heart rate is:

(220 − 35) − 70 × 60 + 70 = 139 beats per minute

Table 6:3 HOW TO ASSESS YOUR FITNESS LEVEL

Level 1—Previously totally inactive.

Level 2—Previously sedentary (exercised occasionally).

Level 3—Previously active (exercised on weekends and occasionally during weekdays).

Level 4—Previously very active (maintained fitness and exercised at least three to four times a week).

Level 5—Previously elite athlete or competitor (exercised almost daily to improve performance).

Table 6:4 BORG'S RATING OF PERCEIVED EXERTION (RPE) SCALE

6	
7	very, very light
8	
9	very light
10	
11	fairly light
12	
13	somewhat hard
14	
15	hard
16	
17	very hard
18	
19	very, very hard

Table 6:5 GUIDELINES FOR AN EXERCISE PRESCRIPTION

Fitness level	1–2	3–4	5*
Frequency (days per week)	3	3–4	5
Intensity (maximum heart rate)	110–140	140	140 + *
Time (minutes of continuous exercise)	10–20	20 (mild) 40 (moderate)	less than 60 min.

*Requires medical clearance and/or supervision.
(Types of exercises are listed in the following schedule.)

■ **Recommended Daily Allowance (RDA) for Physical Activity and Exercise during Pregnancy**

Before designing specific exercise regimens, it's important to emphasize general guidelines. These are:

1. *Frequency of training.* Regular exercise three to five times a week is preferable to infrequent sessions. (It is not necessary to exercise more than five times a week to derive health benefits, even in the nonpregnant state.) Regular, more moderate activities such as brisk walking, swimming, or modified calisthenics promote fitness as well as muscle strength and tone and retain mobility with little or no risk. A significant reduction in aerobic-fitness capacity occurs after only two weeks of inactivity. During pregnancy, competitive activities should be discouraged. For example, a marathon run or any track and field competition can result in injuries to your baby and to you.

2. *Intensity.* Exercise during pregnancy preferably should be moderate (12 to 14 on the RPE Scale), with a maximum heart rate of 140 beats per minute. This is sufficient to derive health benefits and aerobic fitness, even in nonpregnant women, and to minimize the risk of injuries. If you don't want to stop to take your pulse, you can do the "talk test": If you cannot converse normally while exercising, you're overdoing.

3. *Duration of training or exercise.* Fifteen to twenty minutes of continuous, moderately intense exercise, such as brisk walking, light jogging, or cycling at a low-resistance setting is sufficient. You can, however, resume exercise after resting for ten minutes or so. In general, however, you should avoid exercising continuously in excess of forty-five minutes, since this could dangerously lower your blood sugar (glucose), the body's major source of energy. To maintain or improve aerobic fitness in the nonpregnant state, approximately 260 calories should be burned in a session for a 130-pound (60 kilogram) woman or 300 calories for a 154-pound (70 kilogram) woman. These figures should be similar or lower for pregnant women, but since sometimes they cannot be achieved in one continuous daily session, a woman may wish to combine several activities at different times of the day (see Table 6:6). Remember, too, that your body's metabolism increases significantly during pregnancy, and you are likely to feel tired regardless of what you do. Thus, it is essential to set aside some time each day for rest.

Table 6:6 CALORIES CONSUMED DURING VARIOUS PHYSICAL ACTIVITIES

Activity	Calories consumed per hour*
	(for a 150-pound person)
Bed exercise (arm movement, etc.)	100–220
Bicycling	400–600
Bowling	250–500
Calisthenics	370–600
Gardening (lifting, stooping)	500
Golf (walking, carrying bag)	500–750
Handball	660
Jogging (6 mph)	750
Lawn mowing (with push mower)	450
Paddleball/racquetball	750–1,000
Skating (ice or roller)	500–850
Skiing (downhill)	500–850
Skiing (cross-country)	750–1,000
Softball	370–750
Stair climbing	500–800
Swimming (25–50 yards per minute)	360–750
Tennis	500–800
Walking (level surface)	
2 miles per hour	220
3 miles per hour	300
4 miles per hour	420

*Varies according to intensity, with the higher numbers reflecting the more intense activity.

Note: There is an approximate 10 percent increase in caloric consumption for each 15 pounds over 150 pounds and a 10 percent decrease for each 15 pounds under 150 pounds. *Remember, you should not attempt weight reduction during pregnancy through either diet or exercise, since it could seriously jeopardize your health and that of your unborn baby. Note also that this chart lists calories burned per hour; during pregnancy, strenuous exercise sessions should be limited to 15 to 20 minutes.*

Other important points to keep in mind include:

1. Avoid prolonged intense exercise, which raises the maternal core (rectal) temperature. During exercise the body burns more energy (fuel), and burning extra fuel produces heat. (It's comparable to turning up the thermostat on a furnace.) Just thirty to forty-five minutes of intense exercise could raise core temperature to 100.4 degrees F (38 degrees C). Avoid raising your temperature above these levels by limiting continuous vigorous activity to not more than twenty minutes at a time. Also, avoid exercising in hot, humid weather or if you have a fever.
2. Drink plenty of cool fluids.
3. Consume adequate calories to meet your energy needs as well as those of the fetus. In general, a pregnant woman needs an extra three hundred calories a day, and proportionately more if she exercises regularly. (After delivery, if you elect to breast-feed, you need an extra four hundred to five hundred calories a day.)

■ Designing Your Own Exercise Regimen

Most women can easily determine what's best for them by simply using common sense. Still, before embarking on an exercise program you should discuss it with your obstetrician. This is especially important if you are in a high-risk group.

Your exercise program can be individualized. There are no absolute rules other than those covered in the section on general guidelines. It's important to pick an activity or activities that you enjoy. For example, swimming is an ideal exercise during pregnancy, but if you hate being in water then it makes little sense to build your exercise program around swimming.

A balanced program will achieve changes primarily in the cardiorespiratory system. Overdoing or exercising in a wrong manner may achieve the opposite effect, since injury may preclude most activities. It is important to recognize that good muscle tone is needed to improve the quality of exercise; thus, an exercise routine should work the body's large muscles to achieve well-toned muscles. Activities that achieve this goal include swimming, brisk walking, biking, jogging, and other similar activities that involve large muscles. To maintain flexibility, the exercise routine should include all joints and their full range of motion (see specific exercise programs in Chapter 7). Remember that because of the changes of pregnancy, your joints and the ligaments that support them may be more lax than normal and more vulnerable to injuries. Thus, the repetition of each movement should be kept at comfortable levels, usually ten or fewer. If you add a weight load it should be no more than five or six pounds.

When planning an exercise routine to maintain or improve flexibility, be sure to include the hip. The hip is one joint that usually does not achieve a full range of motion. (See pp. 104–110 for modified calisthenics that exercise the hip.) Squatting promotes flexibility and strength of the knees. Climbing stairs or bicycling improves the strength of both the knees and hips.

During pregnancy, changes may occur in your spinal curvature, and it is particularly important to protect your back and strengthen the abdominal muscles. Some of the exercises illustrated in Chapter 7 are designed specifically for this purpose. Resistance training with light weights also achieves this, but caution is needed to avoid injury during pregnancy. Exercise programs that involve resistance or weight training should be supervised by a qualified instructor, such as a physical therapist.

Your fitness program should include a simple stretching routine, but don't overdo it. As stressed repeatedly throughout this book, pregnancy brings a loosening of joints and ligaments, and excessive stretching may result in injury.

If an exercise produces discomfort, *do not do it*. As you gain weight and your center of gravity shifts, activities that were once enjoyable may produce discomfort. For example, many dedicated joggers find that as their pregnancies advance jogging is no longer comfortable. If this happens to you, you may have to modify your routine or switch to a less demanding activity. Brisk walking, stationary cycling, or swimming can achieve the same cardiovascular and exercise benefits, but without as much trauma to joints and ligaments.

■ *How to Monitor Yourself*

We cannot overemphasize the need to take extra precautions to make sure you don't overdo your exercise program and deprive the fetus of vital oxygen. Start by choosing an appropriate exercise activity you like.

There are several easy methods to determine whether you are overdoing. One is the talk test described earlier—if you can speak normally without gasping for breath while exercising, you are probably exercising within a safe range.

Another is using what is called the RPE or Rate of Perceived Exertion Scale. This scale ranges from 6 (resting state) to 19 (maximal exercise). In general, your perception of exertion correlates with increased heart rate and other manifestations of vigorous activity. During pregnancy exercise should be limited to what is perceived as moderate.

Another widely recommended self-monitoring tactic is to stop now and then to take your pulse. You can do this by pressing your index and middle fingers lightly against the spot on your neck—just to the side of your Adam's apple—where you can feel your pulse. Or place these same fingers on your wrist's pulse point. Using a watch with a second hand, count every pulsation you feel for fifteen seconds. If your pulse rate registers more than about 35 beats per fifteen seconds, or 140 beats per minute, you are exercising too rigorously and need to rest until your heart rate drops to 22 beats per fifteen seconds or less than 90 beats per minute. Then you can gradually resume exercising.

To make sure that your core temperature is in the safe range, you may want to take your temperature at the end of an exercise period. Core temperature may be measured either rectally (obviously not very practical when you exercise) or by placing a thermometer in your armpit. Your temperature should not exceed 38 degrees C (or about 101 degrees F). If your body heat rises beyond that point you are exercising too hard and need to moderate your routine. It is not necessary to constantly monitor your temperature. By measuring it on a few occasions you will become familiar with the "feeling" of normal versus how you feel when your temperature is too high. Furthermore, if you exercise within the limits outlined in this book, you are unlikely to reach hazardous temperature levels.

■ *Exercise Programs*

In developing a model exercise program it's important to remember that:

■ Any program or activity that you choose should be simple, involve large muscles, include a full range of motion, and be enjoyable. If you don't enjoy an exercise program chances are you will abandon it rather quickly. We recognize that the acceptable jargon for exercise programs is "workout," but "funout" might be a more appropriate and effective approach.

■ An exercise session should consist of three phases. Each session should begin with warm-up exercises that emphasize slow, full range of movements and *light* stretching (a dozen examples are illustrated in the Selected Calisthenics section in Chapter 7). Allocate five to ten minutes of your total exercise program to a warm-up. When you free yourself of muscular tightness and you feel "loose," you are adequately warmed up and ready to exercise. For beginners or even for the more athletically inclined, the exercise routine itself may be an extension of the warm-up period.

■ End each session with a cool-down period. This also should take approximately five to ten minutes. Sudden cessation of exercise may cause discomfort, including dizziness caused by a pooling of blood in the legs. When you do cool-down exercises be sure to move around. Simply walking at a slow pace for a few minutes is all that is needed.

Both the warm-up and cool-down sessions are necessary to prevent or reduce the risk of injury, to balance the muscle activity, and to acclimatize the cardiovascular system for exercise and then allow for its recovery to a normal heart rate.

Table 6:7 MODEL EXERCISE SCHEDULE

There is no ideal exercise program, and you may have to modify any program to meet your individual needs. This schedule should be considered only a broad model that you can adapt as you like. You may want to vary your activities, walking one day, cycling the next, and then swimming or doing calisthenics. Try, however, to exercise at least three times per week, preferably on alternating days (for example, Sunday, Tuesday, Thursday, and Saturday) rather than on consecutive days.

Exercise	Monday	Tuesday	Wednesday	Thursday	Friday	Saturday	Sunday
Walking (4 mph) 30–45 min.		x		x		x	
Rest day	x		x		x		x
Swimming 20 min.	x		x		x		x
Rest day		x		x		x	
Stationary cycling 20 min.		x		x			x
Rest day	x		x		x	x	
Calisthenics 30 min.	x		x		x		x
Rest day		x		x		x	
Jogging (6 mph) 20 min.		x		x		x	
Rest day	x		x		x		x

7

HOW TO DESIGN
YOUR OWN
EXERCISE PROGRAM

In previous chapters we have discussed the effects of exercise on a woman's body and emphasized the importance of *moderate* physical activity during pregnancy. Now it's time to design a step-by-step exercise program that you can safely follow throughout your pregnancy.

▪ *Specific Exercise Recommendations*

After you understand the general exercise guidelines outlined in the previous chapter, you are ready to tackle the issue of what specific exercises may or may not be appropriate for you during pregnancy. Basically, such activities fall into three broad categories: cardioregspiratory endurance (also known as "aerobic" exercises); muscular strength and endurance; and nonaerobic flexibility exercises.

Remember the three stages of exercise:

1. A ten-minute warm-up.
2. The exercise period.
3. A ten-minute cool-down.

Cardiorespiratory Endurance Activities

■ *Walking*

Walking is an excellent exercise for pregnant women because it helps improve cardiovascular conditioning while rarely stressing the mother's body or the fetus. Many obstetricians consider regular, brisk walking the best physical activity for most of their pregnant patients. Even if you

■ DO'S AND DON'TS CHECKLIST FOR WALKING

- It is safe to begin a walking program even after you become pregnant.
- Begin with slow walks, then gradually increase your routine to a brisk, twenty- to thirty-minute walk at least three times a week.
- Keep your pace steady and let your arms swing naturally at your sides.
- Walk with a normal gait. The exaggerated gait of race walking increases the risk of orthopedic injury during pregnancy.
- Wear comfortable walking shoes that offer good support.
- When it is hot and humid, use the same precautions that apply to jogging or any other physical activity.

were sedentary before you became pregnant, we recommend beginning a low-intensity walking program during pregnancy.

Ambling along as if you were window-shopping, however, won't help much when it comes to maintaining cardiovascular fitness. Instead, try walking at a moderate to brisk pace every day, gradually increasing your exercise routine to twenty- to thirty-minute sessions.

■ *Bicycling*

Bicycling, particularly on a stationary cycle, is also a fine exercise for pregnant women. In fact, studies suggest that a moderate cycling program can be undertaken even after pregnancy has begun.

Yet even bicycling has its health risks. If you cycle outdoors in traffic and smog, you may be exposing yourself and the fetus to harmful pollutants. If you ride a ten-speed and have to lean forward to grasp the handlebars, you can strain your lower back. (You can reduce this risk by simply sitting up straighter and doing other exercises to strengthen your abdomen.) What's more, uneven terrain and your own uneven weight distribution can increase the risk of falling. And, of course, excessive cycling carries the same risks for the fetus as excessive jogging or any other exercise.

To eliminate many of these risks we recommend using a stationary bicycle. But even this activity must be monitored carefully so that you do not overdo it and push your body temperature up too high.

■ DO'S AND DON'TS CHECKLIST FOR BICYCLING

- If you wish you can begin moderate cycling or switch from jogging or other exercise to cycling after you become pregnant.
- Avoid cycling out-of-doors when humidity and temperature are high or in areas containing high concentrations of air pollutants.
- Sit as straight as possible to avoid low back pain.
- Try a stationary bicycle in order to avoid falls that might result from poor terrain and the body's uneven weight distribution.

■ *Swimming*

Since swimming is a non-weight-bearing aerobic activity, it is an excellent exercise to maintain physical fitness during pregnancy. The changing composition of your body makes you more buoyant and the activity easier. The ideal water temperature should be between 83 and 86 degrees F (28 and 30 degrees C). Exposure to water cooler than 83 degrees F may result in shivering, and if the water is warmer than 98.4 degrees F (36 degrees C), it could raise the body's core temperature (hyperthermia). Most swimming pools are maintained at about 83 to 85 degrees F (28 to 29 degrees C).

Swimming poses a few risks during pregnancy, provided, of course, that you are a competent swimmer and have easy access to a pool. During the second and third trimesters, breathing may become more difficult while swimming and this, too, may limit your swimming. As long as you can swim for 15 to 20 minutes, you still can enjoy the benefits of this aerobic workout.

If you are not a good swimmer you might want to substitute water calisthenics or walking-in-water programs for swimming. Both types of programs offer cardiovascular benefits similar to swimming. You can also do childbirth preparatory exercises in water; not only does the water offer enough resistance to make you expend adequate energy, but it also buoys you up to make exercising easier.

When swimming, attempt to keep your back straight.

■ **DO'S AND DON'TS CHECKLIST FOR SWIMMING**

- Do not swim in water that's either too hot (more than 98 degrees F) or too cold (less than 83 degrees F).
- Avoid swimming so strenuously that your heart rate increases to more than 140 beats per minute. Remember the RPE Scale.
- If respiratory changes make swimming difficult late in pregnancy, switch to water calisthenics.
- For safety, avoid swimming where there are high waves or a strong undertow.
- Avoid hot tubs or whirlpool baths in water that exceeds 38.5 C or 101 degrees F. As stressed earlier, such high temperatures may harm the fetus.

■ *Jogging*

Millions of American women jog, enjoying the many health benefits such aerobic exercise offers. Once you become pregnant, however, you need to take extra care if you want to continue your jogging routine.

During the first trimester, for example, you should pay careful attention to your body's reaction to exercise. Take notice if you feel nauseated, vomit, or gain an insufficient amount of weight. These may be warning signs that you should shorten your distance and/or slow your pace. Be aware, too, that such potentially harmful conditions as ketosis (an upset in body chemistry caused by overly rapid breakdown of body fat) and hypoglycemia (low blood sugar) also may occur during rigorous exercise.

Don't push yourself too hard. If you're experiencing morning sickness and/or fatigue, common symptoms of the first trimester, you may want to consider switching to walking or shortening your distance. In fact, during the first twelve weeks of pregnancy it's best to run no more than one and one-half to two miles per day, especially if the temperature outside is warm. Running for longer distances in warm or humid weather could increase your core body temperature and prevent dissipation of fetal heat. If your temperature rises too high and/or you start to feel dizzy or faint, gradually stop exercising until you cool down (when your breathing and heart rate return to normal). You could be experiencing heat stress or exhaustion that could cause severe fetal deformities or pregnancy loss.

Your second and third trimesters present other problems that may dissuade you from jogging as your pregnancy progresses. Increased body weight may make running difficult. You may also experience some swelling of the legs, varicose veins, or joint laxity produced by hormonal and connective-tissue changes. Such conditions can put you at higher risk for injury than before you became pregnant. In some cases, joint laxity can lead to impairment of your gross motor coordination, which can also heighten your chances of injury.

Don't become so discouraged that you give up, however; instead, modify your physical activities to suit your individual needs.

Despite the cautions, the good word is that research shows you can continue jogging during these trimesters without compromising your own health or that of the fetus so long as you limit your distance. Studies involving pregnant joggers show that when they reduced the number of miles jogged from 2.5 miles three times a week in the first trimester to 1.75 miles in the second trimester and one mile in the third, or maintained a level of about 1.5 miles throughout, they were able to continue their exercise routine without increasing health risks.

■ DO'S AND DON'TS CHECKLIST FOR JOGGING

- To be safest, reduce running distance to less than two miles per day.
- If, during the first trimester, you wish to run more than two miles per day, consult with your physician.
- Do not jog when temperature and humidity are high.
- Pay careful attention to running terrain to avoid injury.
- Do not initiate a jogging program after you become pregnant. Only women who have jogged regularly prior to pregnancy are candidates for a running program during pregnancy.

Running competitively, that is, at high speeds or for long distances should be discontinued when you're pregnant. Instead, concentrate on running to maintain general health and cardiovascular fitness. If you are a professional or elite athlete you may engage in strenuous physical activities to maintain and improve performance, but only under strict medical supervision (recognizing that the risks then become a judgment call). This will ensure that if you or your baby experience adverse side effects, they can be promptly treated. Remember, some of the best-known pregnant athletes have had to curtail or modify their exercise routines because of pregnancy-related changes.

■ *Aerobic Dancing*

It's understandable that many fitness-conscious women enjoy participating in aerobic-dancing programs and why, when they become pregnant, they are reluctant to give up these workouts. Aerobics combines the movement of dance with the fun and support of group workouts while maintaining or improving participants' cardiovascular fitness as well.

In fact, more and more pregnant women who want to continue doing aerobics are attending classes designed for their special needs. You should be aware, however, that to date no studies have assessed the safety of high-impact aerobics during pregnancy. All too often, aerobics classes are led by persons who are not qualified to design safe exercise programs for pregnant women.

If you do choose to participate in aerobics-for-pregnancy classes, make certain you first consult with your physician and select a program developed and supervised by a qualified exercise professional, physical therapist, and obstetrician. Remember, too, that aerobics, like jogging, can put you at risk for various health hazards, including heat stress, fetal distress, and joint and ligament problems. It is important, then, to have yourself tested during each trimester to see how you and the fetus are responding to the aerobic workouts.

■ **DO'S AND DON'TS CHECKLIST FOR AEROBIC DANCING**

- Select a program created and supervised by qualified health-care professionals.
- Warm up and cool down gradually.
- Do not overextend muscles (and risk injuries).
- If you do aerobics with a videotape, follow the same precautions in your selections as for an aerobics class. The American College of Obstetricians and Gynecologists has prepared a videotape, which is the one we recommend to our patients. A few other programs are available; check with your obstetrician before using them.
- Avoid exercises performed while lying on your back.

■ *Selected Calisthenics*

There are any number of simple calisthenics that can be combined into a balanced exercise routine. The exercises illustrated on the following pages are designed to safely work all of the major muscle groups. When done in order, they provide a complete workout. Alternatively, some may be used as warm-up and cool-down exercises before and after walking, cycling, swimming, or other physical activity.

WALKING WARM-UP

Objective/goal: To prepare muscles for exercise, warm up all large muscles, prevent injuries, and reduce muscle soreness. May alleviate muscle strains and low back pain. It should not be carried to extreme.

How to do it: Start from normal standing position with arms relaxed. Raise one leg to 90 degrees and swing opposite arm to and fro. Repeat with opposite side.

Frequency: Beginning and end of each session.

Duration: One minute of walking in place and 3 to 5 minutes of normal walking around the room.

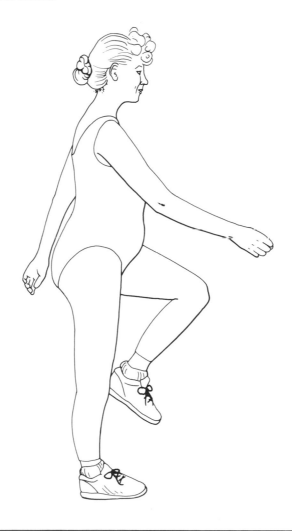

LIGHT ARM STRETCHES

Objective/goal: Stretch the arm and continue to warm up upper body muscles.

How to do it: Stand comfortably with feet 6 to 8 inches apart, knees relaxed. Bring arms to shoulder height with hands clasped; extend arms fully in front of you, but do not lock elbows.

Frequency: Each exercise session.

Duration: 10 repetitions.

BUTTERFLY MOTION

Objective/goal: Strengthen and stretch muscles of the upper chest and shoulders.

How to do it: Stand erect with legs astride. Bend elbows and place fingertips on shoulders. On the count of 3, move elbows from chest to about 90 degrees, keeping fingertips in place.

Frequency: Part of each exercise session.

Duration: 10 repetitions.

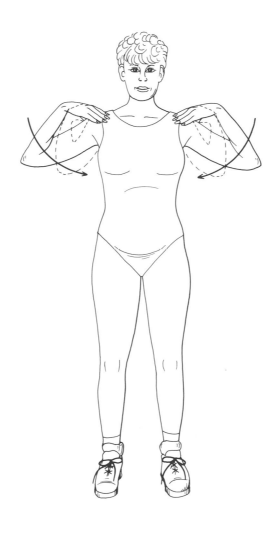

TRANSITIONAL SIDE STRETCH

Objective/goal: To activate major muscles. Transitional—to stretch the lateral muscles of the trunk and chest and the muscles of the thigh.

How to do it: Stand astride with legs about 18 inches apart and knees relaxed (avoid locking knees). Raise left arm over head and right side. Bend trunk to the right, extending left arm until you feel a slight pulling along upper body. Lower arm and repeat with opposite side.

Frequency: Each exercise session.

Duration: 10 repetitions.

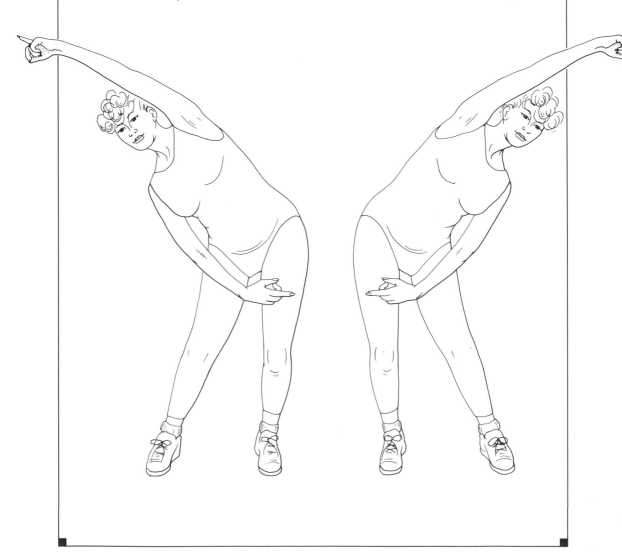

TRUNK ROTATIONS

Objective/goal: To stretch muscles of the trunk.
How to do it: Stand comfortably with feet 6 to 8 inches apart. (Avoid locking knees.) Bring arms to shoulder height with elbows bent and fingers touching the shoulders. Rotate trunk to the left and then back to the right.
Frequency: Each exercise session.
Duration: 10 repetitions.

UPPER BODY BENDS

Objective/goal: To strengthen back and upper and lower torso.
How to do it: Start from an erect position with legs astride, knees slightly bent (unlocked), and hands resting on hips. Keeping upper back straight, slowly bend forward. You should feel a slight pulling along upper thigh.
Frequency: Each exercise session.
Duration: 10 repetitions.

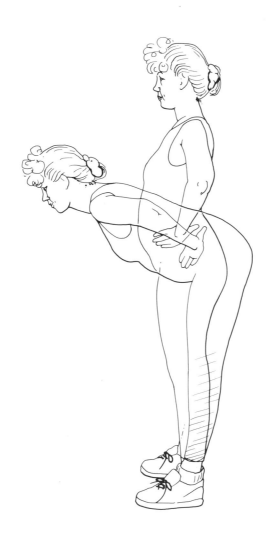

TRANSITION TO TRUNK MUSCLES—HALF BENDS

Objective/goal: To strengthen lower back.
How to do it: Stand with legs astride, knees slightly bent, and hands on hips. Bend forward 90 degrees or less, with back straight. Rotate upper body from side to side.
Frequency: Each exercise session.
Duration: 10 repetitions.

ARM RAISES

Objective/goal: Lightly stretch and tone shoulder, upper back, and trunk muscles.

How to do it: Stand with legs astride, knees loose, and both arms at side with palms extended. Raise arms over head until hands cross in a swinging motion. Lower arms sideways and down until arms cross in front. Both raising and lowering of arms should be done slowly.

Frequency: Each exercise session.

Duration: 10 repetitions.

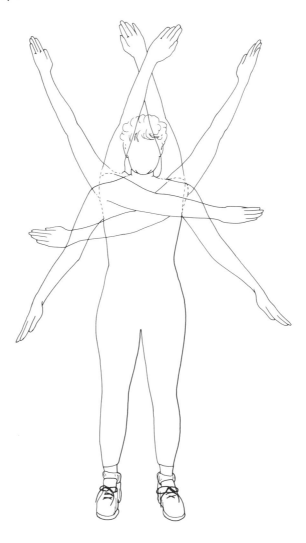

WARM-UP WITH WEIGHTS

Objective/goal: Strengthen shoulder, upper back, and arm muscles.
How to do it: Stand comfortably with legs astride and knees relaxed. Grip a 2- to 6-pound weight in right hand with arm straight, but elbow unlocked. Slowly lift weight to shoulder height. Lower slowly and repeat with left hand.
Frequency: Prior to each exercise session.
Duration: 10 repetitions.

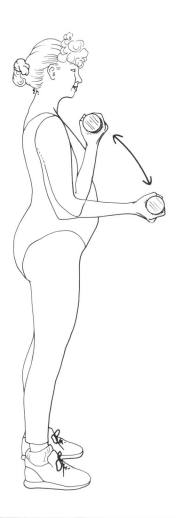

BACK AND LOWER LEG STRETCH

Objective/goal: Strengthen lower leg muscles.
How to do it: Stand with legs and feet slightly apart on a step with heels extended a couple of inches. Raise on toes. Begin this exercise slowly since it is easy to overstretch and injure the leg muscles.
Frequency: With each exercise session.
Duration: 10 repetitions.

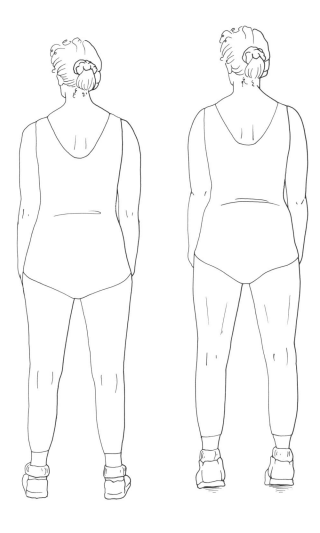

STANDING PELVIC TILT

Objective/goal: To strengthen abdominal wall and lower back muscles.
How to do it: Stand comfortably with arms at your side, feet 4 or 5 inches apart, and knees slightly bent. Squeeze buttocks and abdominal muscles and thrust the pelvis gently forward while rotating the pubic bone upward. Hold for 10 seconds and release.
Frequency: Each exercise session.
Duration: 10 repetitions.

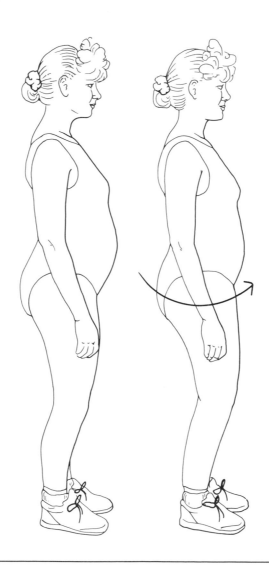

BACK PRESS

Objective/goal: To strengthen back, trunk, and upper body and to correct lordosis (swayback).

How to do it: Stand with back against a wall with feet 10 to 12 inches away from base of wall. Press lower part of back against wall. Hold for a count of 10 and release.

Frequency: Each exercise session.

Duration: 10 repetitions.

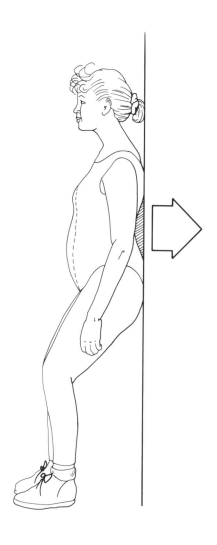

FORWARD BEND

Objective/goal: To stretch and strengthen back muscles.

How to do it: Sit comfortably in a chair with arms relaxed. Slowly bend forward, with arms extending down. Do not force yourself if you feel discomfort or abdominal pressure. Count to 5 and rise slowly without arching back.

Frequency: Each exercise session.

Duration: 5 repetitions.

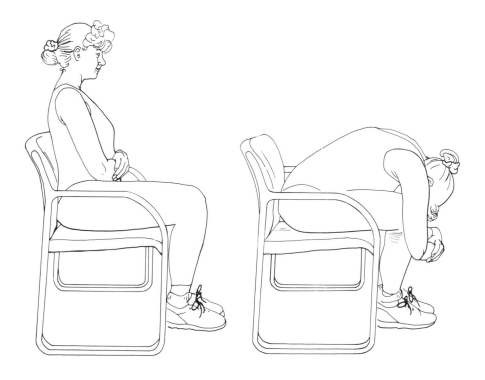

MODIFIED SQUATTING

Objective/goal: To strengthen thigh, gluteal, and back muscles.

How to do it: Stand astride with feet flat and hip-width apart. With both hands grip back of chair positioned in front of you. Holding on to chair back, raise on toes a couple of inches. Squat slowly with hands gripping chair until buttocks touch heels (unless this produces pain). Count to 5, and rise slowly.

Frequency: Each exercise session.

Duration: 5 to 10 repetitions.

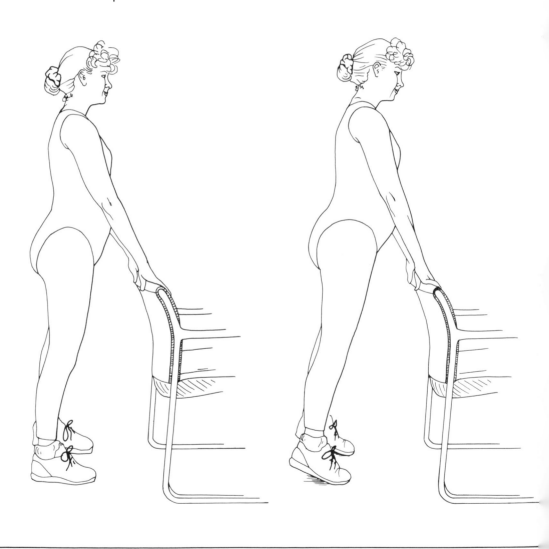

SEATED LEG LIFTS

Objective/goal: Strengthen upper legs.
How to do it: Can be done with or without weights (up to 5 lbs.). Flex toes, raise and extend leg. Count to 5 and lower.
Frequency: With each exercise session.
Duration: 10 repetitions.

DIAGONAL CURL

(Advanced exercise for athletic women only.)
Objective/goal: To strengthen back, hip, and abdominal muscles.
How to do it: Sit on floor with knees bent and hands clasped. Twist upper body until clasped hands touch floor on one side; repeat on opposite side.
Frequency: Each session.
Duration: 5 times.

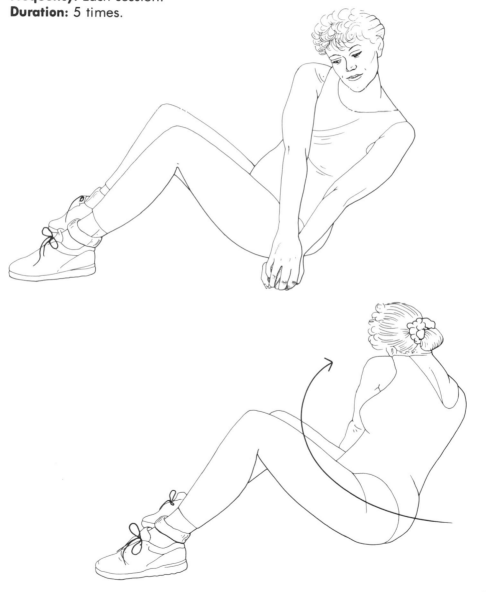

TRUNK TWIST

Objective/goal: To stretch back, spine, and upper trunk muscles.
How to do it: Sit with legs crossed and left hand gripping opposite foot.
Support yourself with right hand. Slowly twist upper body to the right.
Repeat on opposite side.
Frequency: Each exercise session.
Duration: 5 to 10 repetitions.

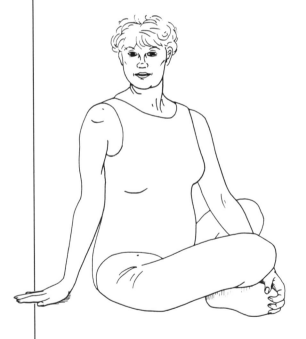
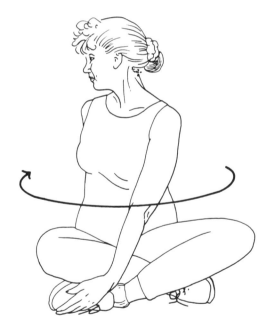

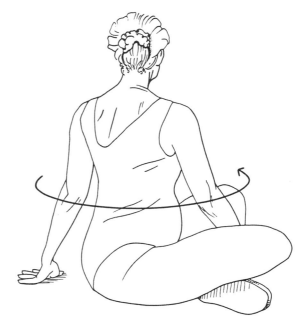

SIT-BACKS

(Advanced exercise for athletic women only—requires good abdominal strength.)
Objective/goal: To strengthen back and abdominal muscles.
How to do it: Sit on floor with knees bent and hands crossed over upper chest. Tuck chin down and slowly lean backward, but not enough to fall over. Shift crossed hands down to abdomen. Move back up to full sitting position.
Frequency: Each exercise session.
Duration: 5 times.

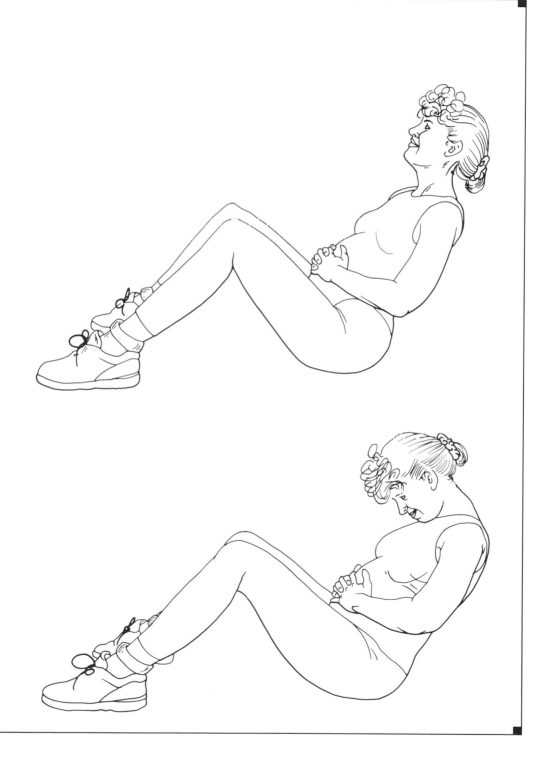

DONKEY STRETCH

Objective/goal: To gently stretch and strengthen back, pelvic, and thigh muscles.

How to do it: Kneel on all fours with arms extended straight from the shoulders and knees 8 to 10 inches apart. Slowly curl backward, tucking head toward knees while keeping arms extended. Hold for a count of 5, then slowly rise.

Frequency: Each session.

Duration: 5 times.

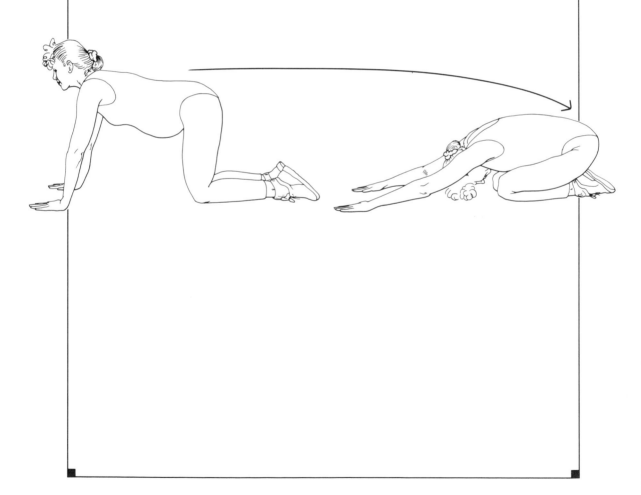

MODIFIED LEG LIFTS

Objective/goal: To strengthen hip and upper leg and thigh muscles.
How to do it: Lie on your side with lower leg bent and upper leg extended and knee unlocked. Raise straight leg about 45 degrees. Next, bend knee and lower leg over one on floor. Try to raise knee to a 90-degree angle. Roll over and repeat on opposite side.
Frequency: Each exercise session.
Duration: 5 times.

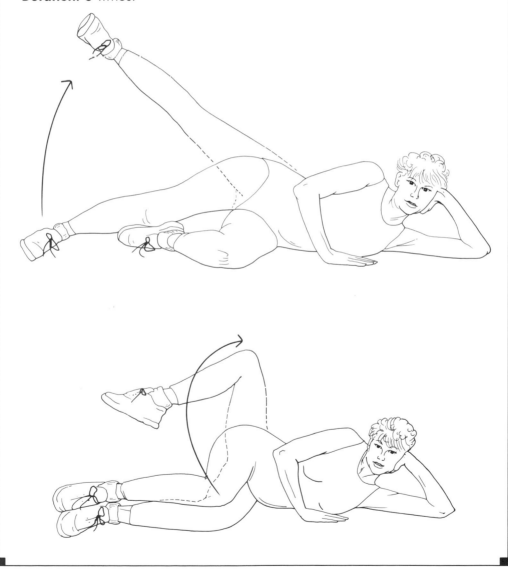

SEATED STRETCH

Objective/goal: To stretch back muscles.
How to do it: Sit cross-legged on the floor with back straight. Slowly raise arms overhead until arms are straight. Bend forward with head between the arms. Bring head toward knees and attempt to touch the floor with outstretched hands. Count to 5 and slowly return to sitting position.
Frequency: Each session.
Duration: 5 times.

LEG-LIFT CRAWL
(Semi-advanced exercise)

Objective/goal: To strengthen back and abdominal muscles, and to correct lordosis.

How to do it: Kneel on all fours with weight evenly distributed. On a count of 5, lift one knee and bring forward toward elbow. Then straighten leg without locking knee and extend upward and backward. Move slowly and evenly; avoid "flinging" leg backward and arching back. Alternate with opposite leg.

Frequency: Each exercise session.

Duration: 5 to 10 repetitions.

ROCKING BACK ARCH

Objective/goal: To strengthen and stretch hip, back, and abdominal muscles, and to correct lordosis.

How to do it: Kneel on all fours with weight evenly distributed, and with back straight. To a count of five, rock back and forth. Return to original position and arch back as much as possible.

Frequency: Each exercise session.

Duration: 5 to 10 repetitions.

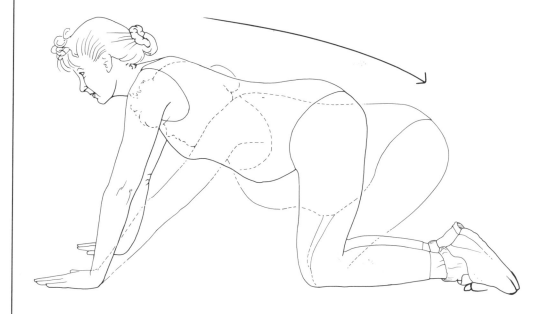

GROIN EXERCISES

Objective/goal: To stretch and strengthen groin.
How to do it: Sit with knees bent outward and soles pointed toward each other. Place hands on thighs just above knee and gently press downward. Hold for a count of 5.
Frequency: Each exercise session.
Duration: 5 to 10 repetitions.

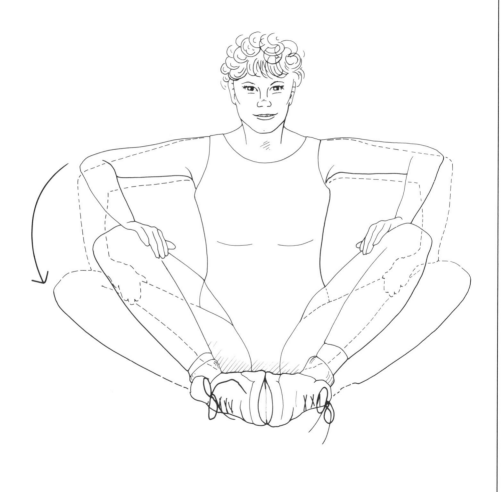

COOL DOWN

Cool down by repeated walking at a slow pace. Check pulse by placing 2 fingers gently over carotid artery in the neck, just below and to the side of the jaw. Count beats for 15 seconds and multiply by 4 to get your heart rate in beats per minute.
(Note: Avoid exerting pressure on the carotid artery. Alternative pulse points are in the temple, the elbow, and the wrist.)

Muscular Strength and Endurance Activities

■ *Weight Lifting*

Weight lifting is not an activity we recommend for pregnant women. This exercise, especially when performed lying on your back, can result in compression of the abdominal blood vessels and reduced blood supply to the fetus. Strenuous workouts divert blood to the mother's working muscles to a greater extent than any other activity.

If, however, you have been lifting weights regularly prior to your pregnancy, you may continue during pregnancy, *provided* you use light weights and work out under the strict supervision of a qualified health professional. Switching from heavy to very light weights is important in preventing injuries to ligaments that normally loosen during pregnancy. Proper breathing—exhaling while doing a lift and inhaling while releasing or resting—is also critical to reduce any excess stress. When using resistance or weight machines, limit the resistance to neutral or light weights of 4.4 to 11 pounds (2 to 5 kilograms).

■ DO'S AND DON'TS CHECKLIST FOR WEIGHT LIFTING

- Do not initiate a weight-lifting regimen after you become pregnant.
- Exercise extreme caution if continuing a program in which you have already been participating.
- Use only light weights.
- Avoid the use of free weights.
- Concentrate on proper breathing techniques.
- Don't lift weights or exercise while lying on your back.
- Consult with your physician and exercise in a well-supervised program.

In any case, avoid any regimen that requires you to lie on your back. Again, lifting weights during pregnancy should be limited and done only under the advice of your doctor and the supervision of a health-care professional.

Sample Exercise Routines

You can easily put together your own exercise routine using a selection of exercises from the section on calisthenics as warm-up and cool-down exercises. When making your selection, be sure that you pick a variety to put all your joints through a full range of motion.

▪ *Walking*

Frequency: three or four times a week, preferably on alternating days.
Duration: twenty to thirty minutes.
Intensity: Maintain a moderately brisk pace of four miles per hour (or a pace that feels comfortably brisk to you). Walk at a smooth, even pace with arms swinging at your side.

Special benefits:

- Can be maintained throughout pregnancy.
- Does not require special equipment other than comfortable walking shoes and a safe place in which to walk.

■ *Warm-up Exercises (Before Walking)*

Light Arm Stretches and Light Leg Stretches
Objective/goal: Stretch and warm upper and lower body muscles.
Frequency: Before each session.
Duration: Five to ten repetitions.

Sports Activities

Many sports are safe during pregnancy, but some pose risks to pregnant women. It is therefore essential to understand the risks, weigh them carefully, and decide whether you should modify or discontinue participating in a given sport once you become pregnant. Here follow our recommendations for today's most popular sports.

We generally *do not* recommend participation in the following, especially during the second and third trimesters of pregnancy.

■ Scuba diving. Diving gear may restrict circulation; decompression sickness (the bends) may harm the fetus.
■ Water skiing and platform diving. Blunt trauma to the abdomen may result from a dive or if you fall when water skiing.
■ High-altitude mountain climbing. The insufficient amounts of oxygen available at high altitudes can stress you and the fetus and result in hypoxia (low concentrations of oxygen in the body).

For the following activities we recommend that participation be limited or that extreme caution be exercised by pregnant women who elect to compete in them:

■ Contact sports, including basketball, hockey, wrestling, or football. The often unpredictable actions of other players and unreliability of equipment increase the risk of abdominal trauma and other injuries.

- Volleyball, gymnastics, and English horsback riding.
- Downhill skiing. There's always a risk of falling. And at altitudes of over ten thousand feet both you and the fetus can be deprived of sufficient oxygen. Excessive cold also can stress your heart and lungs. (If you are an experienced skier or ice skater, you can continue the sport in the early stages of pregnancy, provided you avoid fatigue, strain, and excessive cold or overheating.)

Sports that are generally acceptable include:

- Racket sports, including tennis, racquetball, and squash. These are safe for women who have strong musculature to compensate for the loose joints and ligaments. Take care not to overstretch muscles; this could traumatize joints and ligaments. Also, watch for signs of heat stress.
- Golf. This is a safe activity for pregnant women, although you may have to modify your golf swing to compensate for your extra and redistributed weight.
- Softball. As long as you avoid sliding into and blocking bases and use common sense in moderating your activity, this sport can be enjoyed well into your pregnancy.
- Cross-country skiing. Cross-country skiing provides a good cardiovascular workout and promotes a high level of fitness. However, you should maintain a moderate pace, rest frequently, and drink fluids periodically. Additionally, you should avoid prolonged exposure to extreme cold or overheating.

Nonaerobic Activities

∎ *Yoga*

When supplemented by an aerobic exercise, yoga can provide a good workout for pregnant women, helping to maintain muscle tone, flexibility, and a more relaxed attitude throughout the nine-month period. You may, however, need to modify the yoga postures as your body changes during pregnancy. Since supine and prolonged-standing exercises may induce changes in blood pressure, you should avoid them during pregnancy.

∎ *Preparatory Childbirth Exercises*

Although there is no strong scientific evidence to support popular claims that relaxation and breathing techniques result in fewer birth complications, or shorter, easier labors, toning and stretching exercises may help to speed recovery after you give birth. Learning relaxation techniques may assist you in coping with the pain associated with labor and delivery. Don't be afraid to modify the exercises as your pregnancy progresses. As the abdomen begins protruding, for instance, a half sit-up or sit-back (beginning in the up position and slowly lying down) may be better for you than full sit-ups. In addition, exercising while lying on your back compresses the vena cava, thereby cutting off the return blood supply to your heart and causing hypotension (low blood pressure).

When walking, maintain an even stride, with heel meeting the surface first. Have arms swinging comfortably at your sides. If you feel short of breath or are unable to speak normally, slow down or stop and rest for fifteen minutes.

■ *Cool-down Exercises (After Walking)*

Walk at a slow pace for five to seven minutes to give your breathing and heart rate a chance to return to normal. End the session with five repeats of Butterfly Motion and Standing Pelvic Tilt.

■ PRACTICAL SUGGESTIONS

Several practical suggestions to make your exercise safer and more pleasant:

- Wear comfortable, loose-fitting clothes, athletic-type shoes with good support, and good support hose to maximize your comfort and safety.
- Exercises that include repetitive movements should be done gradually and with moderation.
- Exercise in a well-ventilated room, away from smog, traffic fumes, etc.
- Liquids should be taken liberally prior to and after exercise.
- If in doubt, always consult your physician.

8

EXERCISE FOR SPECIAL CONDITIONS

Certain complications of pregnancy require restriction of physical activities, primarily because of potential adverse effects on the mother and fetus. There are, of course, instances in which pregnancy loss cannot be prevented, no matter what precautions are taken. In other instances, however, the loss may be prevented by complete bed rest or other interventions. (See Table 8:1 for a list of conditions that preclude exercise during pregnancy.)

Although bed rest may be essential to preserve a pregnancy or prevent serious harm to the mother and her fetus, it still has a significant detrimental effect on certain physiological functions. For example, it reduces cardiorespiratory fitness and decreases muscle strength and flexibility. It also carries an increased risk of orthostatic hypotension (dizziness or fainting caused by a sudden drop in blood pressure when

119

going from a lying or sitting to an upright position) and thromboembolism, the formation of blood clots in the deep veins, especially of the legs.

Even if you must stay in bed or are instructed to avoid exercising, there are certain physical activities that can be conducted safely. A word of warning, however: Before doing any of the exercises described in this chapter, *make sure you check with your obstetrician*. Although they are safe for most women, there are exceptions.

Table 8:1 ABSOLUTE CONTRAINDICATIONS FOR
EXERCISE DURING PREGNANCY

History of three or more spontaneous miscarriages.
Rupture of membranes.
Premature labor.
Diagnosed multiple gestation.
Incompetent cervix.
Vaginal bleeding or diagnosis of placenta previa.
Constrictive lung disease.
Diagnosed cardiac disease.
Preeclampsia.

CONDITIONS WITH RELATIVE CONTRAINDICATIONS FOR EXERCISE DURING PREGNANCY

Diabetes.
Hypertension.
Anemia or other blood disorders.
Cardiac arrhythmias or palpitations.
History of precipitous labor.
History of intrauterine growth retardation, resulting in a small-for-age baby.
History of vaginal bleeding during current pregnancy.
Breech presentation in the last trimester.
Seizure disorder.
Chronic bronchitis.
Orthopedic limitations.
Excessive obesity.
Extreme underweight.
History of an extremely sedentary life-style.

The three programs described below may be utilized individually or in a progressive fashion. To do each, the woman should be sitting or in a semisitting position rather than lying supine.

PHASE 1: FOR WOMEN ON COMPLETE BED REST

Exercises should be done two or three times a day:

Passive (with a physical therapist, nurse, or other assistance). Range of motion for all major joints and muscle groups, including slow, large back and forth motions of the arms and legs. Repeat five times.

Isometric (static) exercises. Contract the individual muscles with the limbs extended and flexed for at least six seconds several times a day. For example, tighten the thigh muscles with the knee extended, without using the hip or knee joints. Repeat the contraction with the knee bent.

Caution: Patients with high blood pressure and heart disease should not conduct these activities, since isometric exercise can further increase blood pressure and possibly reduce the supply of oxygen to the heart.

Breathing exercises. Deep, slow breathing several times a day.

PHASE 2: FOR PATIENTS WHOSE CONDITIONS ARE STABLE, BUT WHO STILL MUST BE CONFINED TO BED.

Check with your obstetrician to make sure that range of motion and upright posture shifts are safe. If so, the Phase 1 exercises may be done with the addition of the following calisthenics. (They can be done in any order or combination.)

Flexing of shoulders and abduction
Flexing of elbows
Trunk rotations
Knee extensions
Toe raises
Ankle exercises

PHASE 3: FOR WOMEN WHO CAN GET OUT OF BED FOR CERTAIN PERIODS OF TIME.

Phase 1 and 2 exercises may be done in addition to five minutes of slow walking in the hospital halls or at home, plus up to ten repetitions of muscle-strengthening exercises with a two- to five-pound weight.

■ *Exercise for High-Risk Patients*

In recent years exercise has become an integral part of therapy for various disorders in nonpregnant women. Examples include diabetes, asthma, high blood pressure, and certain other heart or pulmonary disorders. Until recently, however, exercise was not recommended when women with these conditions became pregnant, primarily because doctors feared that any potential benefits to the mother could be offset by increased risks to the fetus. Thus, many of these women spent most of their pregnancies in bed.

This is beginning to change as more is learned about the benefits and risks of exercise. For example, it is now recognized that exercise can play an important role in normalizing blood sugar levels of women with gestational diabetes. It is vital, however, that exercise regimens be worked out by a qualified health professional in collaboration with the woman's obstetrician. In many instances, the exercise should be done under direct supervision.

Many of the principles of exercise guidelines outlined in Chapters 6 and 7 are appropriate for certain high-risk women. The major difference is related to frequency, intensity, and duration of the exercise.

The risks of low-intensity exercise during pregnancy in previously sedentary women (as many patients with diabetes are) are minimal and include mostly soft-tissue musculoskeletal injuries. Thus, non-weight-bearing exercise may be more suitable than weight-bearing activities for these women.

▪ Exercise Programs for the Pregnant Woman with Gestational Diabetes

Several approaches have been described in the medical literature. In one, the eligible patients are enrolled for a one-week trial of exercise and diet to normalize blood sugar levels. If this regimen fails to bring blood sugar into a normal range, the woman is placed on insulin therapy.

In general, the exercise program should last for at least four weeks to give the exercise an opportunity to normalize blood sugar. Patients who are in their thirty-sixth week of pregnancy or later are not enrolled in the exercise program. All exercise sessions are conducted at about fifty percent of each woman's individual maximum aerobic capacity.

Each woman is told how to use home glucose-monitoring devices. Patients are instructed not to exercise if their blood sugar levels are below 60 mg/dl or above 200 mg/dl. Instead, they are to seek immediate medical attention. These patients are also given precautions similar to those listed in Chapter 7.

In our program, patients with gestational diabetes exercise using a recumbent bicycle for a total of forty-five minutes three times a week. Each forty-five-minute session is broken up into three fifteen-minute segments, with five minutes of rest between each one. The woman's blood pressure, heart rate, and blood sugar levels are monitored before, during, and after each exercise session.

The fetal heart rate is also monitored before and after each session. Since babies born to mothers with diabetes have an increased risk of serious complications, they need to be closely monitored.

▪ Home Exercise Programs for Diabetics

The woman is instructed to exercise for twenty minutes after breakfast, lunch, and dinner. She is also told to contact her obstetrician if she has not felt the baby move at least ten times in twenty-four hours.

■ Experimental Programs

It should be stressed that although the potential of exercise as a treatment for gestational diabetes is exciting, the approach is still experimental and thus must be carried out under careful medical supervision. Additional study is needed before it can be established that the approach is safe and effective.

Other experimental programs are assessing the effectiveness of exercise done during early labor to control pain. The goal is to increase the brain's secretion of endorphins, natural pain-killers, and thus avoid the use of pain medication.

9

ORTHOPEDIC PROBLEMS IN PREGNANCY

Physiological changes that take place in the pregnant body significantly affect the musculoskeletal system of the woman. They aggravate most existing orthopedic problems and are likely to trigger new ones, such as leg, knee, and ankle cramps and pain in the lower back and hips. Pregnancy also affects diseases of connective tissue: Certain rheumatological conditions like lupus often worsen during pregnancy, while others, such as rheumatoid arthritis, may improve.

■ *Edema*

An important change that occurs in pregnancy is swelling (edema) of body tissues. In the past, swelling was considered to be a disturbing

125

symptom, but it has been shown that most women have dependent edema while pregnant, particularly in the last eight weeks, and the majority have perfectly normal pregnancies.

Swelling is caused by the retention of fluids in the tissues. This can occur as a result of metabolic changes, but also because the fetus presses on the pelvis and prevents proper circulation of blood and other fluids in the lower body, leading to their buildup in the ankles. Swelling of the lower limbs is most common. Women who must stand for long periods should keep their bodies in motion as much as possible to encourage circulation, or prop up one foot at a time on a stool. While sitting or lying down, the woman should prop up her feet on a footstool, a box, or a firm pillow to help drain fluids from the ankles. Lying on the left side takes the pressure off the inferior vena cava—the large vein that returns blood from the lower part of the body to the heart.

■ CASE STUDY

Mary Ellen is a twenty-eight-year-old grade-school teacher who spends most of her day on her feet. Early in the third trimester of her pregnancy, she noticed that her ankles were so swollen that she could barely fit into her shoes. The swelling worsened as the day progressed. Alarmed that something might be wrong, she went to see her doctor.

Her blood pressure was normal and there was no sign of protein in her urine. The obstetrician advised her that such swelling is normal, especially in light of the fact that she spent so much of her time standing.

"During your free periods," her doctor advised, "try to go to the faculty lounge and rest with your legs elevated. When you go home spend an hour or so lying on your left side. This should help relieve the swelling. You may also want to consider cutting back on your teaching schedule and beginning your maternity leave a few weeks earlier than you had planned."

She followed this advice, asking the school to put her on a three-day-a-week schedule. She also spent her free periods resting as her doctor had instructed. Within a few days the swelling subsided.

Edema is a cause for special concern when it is accompanied by high blood pressure and proteinuria—the excretion of proteins in the urine. The presence of these three symptoms may signal preeclampsia (toxemia), a potentially dangerous condition that can develop in the later part of pregnancy. Women should watch out for swelling in the hands or face and such symptoms as headaches, blurred vision, and/or high abdominal pain, and report these conditions to the doctor immediately.

▪ *Loosening of Tissues*

A second important change affecting orthopedic problems is laxity of the connective tissues (see Fig. 5). It is believed to occur due to increased levels of the hormones estrogen and relaxin during pregnancy.

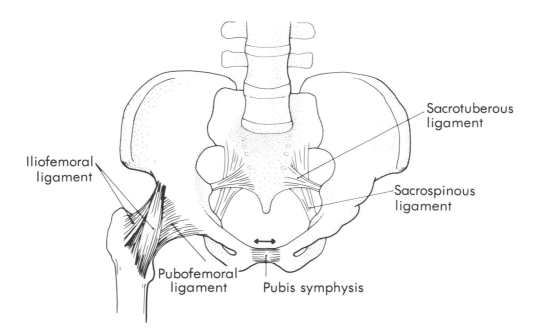

Fig. 5. As pregnancy advances, hormonal changes cause ligaments to loosen in preparation for childbirth. Extra caution is needed to protect against injury to the loosened ligaments.

As a result, the ligaments loosen, and the joints they support become more mobile and prone to sprains. This effect is most pronounced in the pelvis, but it has recently been shown that tissues supporting the feet, fingers and knees also grow looser under the influence of the hormones.

Normally there is no movement whatsoever in the pelvic joint connecting the backbone and the hipbone, but during pregnancy this joint becomes loose and movable to some extent to facilitate the birth of the child. It is this laxity and changes in the center of gravity that are believed to be responsible to a great extent for low back pain in pregnant women.

▪ Weight Gain

An additional change that adds to the stress on the musculoskeletal system of the woman is the increase in body weight that occurs during the later stages of pregnancy. Even though much of this weight gain is from increased body fluids rather than from fat, it still puts an added burden on the joints, which are already weakened by the effect of the hormones. The workload on the joints of the hip and knee, for example, becomes significant even during regular day-to-day activities such as stair climbing. The extra stress may cause injuries in normal joints and exacerbate the existing conditions like arthritis or previous instability.

▪ Weight Distribution

Not only is the body weight increased, but it is distributed unevenly, creating additional problems. As the uterus grows larger and the fetus heavier, the woman's center of gravity is shifted and many of her muscles and joints are placed under additional stress in an effort to counteract the imbalance. The lower back and pelvis are particularly affected as the abdomen grows heavier and pulls forward (see Fig. 6). The new weight distribution also makes the woman less stable and more likely to fall.

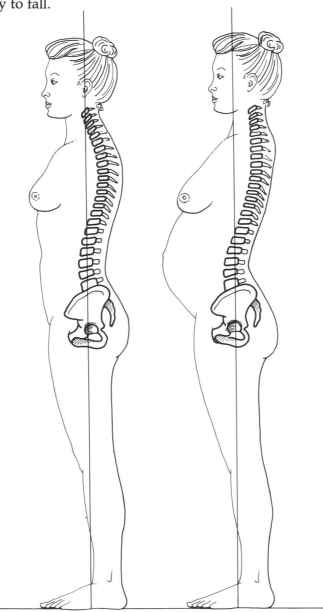

Fig. 6. As pregnancy advances, the body's center of gravity shifts markedly.

■ COMMON EXERCISE-RELATED INJURIES

ANKLE PROBLEMS

Causes: Usually the result of abrupt change in direction.

Treatment: Initial treatment, especially for a sprained ankle, consists of rest, application of an ice pack (not to exceed twenty minutes per session) to prevent swelling, compression, and elevation.

BLISTERS

Causes: These are usually related to new shoes or improperly fitting shoes and socks.

Treatment: Puncture the blister with a sterile needle; gently express the fluid and apply a topical antiseptic such as hydrogen peroxide; cover with gauze.

BONE BRUISES

Causes: These usually occur on the bottom of the feet and are the result of an improper gait.

Treatment: Ice, rest, and padding.

MUSCLES CRAMPS AND SORENESS

Causes: Inadequate warm-up and cool-down exercises.

Treatment: Massage, warm compresses, and gentle flexing of muscles.

SHIN SPLINTS

Causes: Inflammation, swelling, and irritation of the membranes and muscle attachments in the lower leg, resulting in sharp pain in the legs. Also may be caused by hairline or stress fractures or injury to the lower arch of the foot.

Treatment: Rest and wrapping or taping of the leg.

Nerve-compression Syndromes

Accumulated fluids and swollen tissues can cause nerve-compression syndromes by pressing on nerves that pass through limited spaces between ligaments and bones. Similar problems can arise due to pressure exerted by the uterus and fetus and the weight of the enlarging breasts.

■ Carpal Tunnel Syndrome

The carpal tunnel is the space on the inner side of the wrist formed by the wristbone (carpus) and a fibrous ligament just under the skin. The median nerve that travels along the arm passes through the carpal tunnel before it reaches the thumb and the index and middle fingers. It activates the muscles of the palm at the base of the thumb, allowing the thumb to oppose the fingers. Compression of the median nerve at the level of the wrist is known as carpal tunnel syndrome.

The syndrome occurs in typists and other persons whose work places a strain on the wrist, but it is also common during the last trimester of pregnancy. Symptoms include numbness and a tingling sensation in the thumb, index, and middle fingers, loss of thumb

---

■ CASE STUDY

Sarah, a twenty-six-year-old computer programmer, was six months pregnant with her first baby. Her job entailed six to eight hours of computer typing a day. As her pregnancy advanced, so did her problem with carpal tunnel syndrome. By the time she left work each day she experienced tingling and numbness in her hands and shooting pains up her arms. She found it difficult to hold things, and the pain was especially bothersome at night.

Her obstetrician referred her to an orthopedist for an evaluation and treatment. This physician examined her wrist and arms and found mild inflammation. She advised that Sarah wear a wrist splint at night and that she apply ice packs to her wrist during the day. She also recommended that Sarah alter her typing posture a bit, placing the keyboard in her lap so that she could better support her wrists. This regimen relieved Sarah's symptoms within a few days and she was able to continue working until her scheduled maternity leave.

function, and pain that gets worse at night and can awaken the woman from sleep. Discomfort can be relieved only by shaking the hands.

In nonpregnant patients the condition can be treated by taking an occasional anti-inflammatory medication. In severe cases an injection of Xylocaine, an anesthetic medication, may be given. Cortisone, an anti-inflammatory steroid medication, may also be injected into the affected area. During pregnancy, however, medications are avoided whenever possible. Instead, treatment involves placing the woman's wrist in an extension splint for sleeping at night and applying ice packs to the area two to three times a day to decrease inflammation. It is also recommended that the woman avoid the hyperflexion posture of the wrist, which tends to diminish the space available in the carpal tunnel. In severe cases symptoms can be effectively relieved by one or two injections of Xylocaine into the space around the nerve.

The symptoms of carpal tunnel syndrome usually disappear completely after delivery. Should they persist two months after pregnancy is over, the woman is advised to consult a physician for an orthopedic evaluation.

■ *Other Nerve-compression Syndromes*

Tingling and numbness in the fourth and fifth fingers are usually due to the compression of the ulnar nerve, which runs beside the inner bone of the forearm. This is a condition similar to carpal tunnel syndrome, but it occurs much less frequently. Treatment is the same as when the median nerve is compressed.

The ulnar nerve may also become compressed at the elbow, behind its bony eminence. This is often due to incorrect sleeping posture, when the head is resting on the area of the elbow. In these cases treatment involving a splint to immobilize the elbow, ice packs, and/or local injection of cortisone is usually highly effective.

Nerves may also become compressed in the tarsal tunnel in the leg—a thick, fibrous layer of tissue at the back of the ankle. Injury to the posterior tibial nerve that passes through this tunnel produces numbness and tingling in the middle section of the foot and some weakness in the toes. As in the case of other compressed nerves, treatment consists of minimizing the movement in the ankle, applying ice packs, and possibly giving injections around the nerve.

Toward the end of pregnancy the fetus puts pressure on the vaginal nerves, causing tingling and a feeling of pressure in the vagina. Usually there is no reason to worry about this sensation and nothing needs to be done about it.

■ Knee Pain

One cause of knee pain during pregnancy may be pressure exerted on the peroneal nerves, which wrap around the small bones on the outer side of the leg near the knee joint. These are important nerves, responsible for flexing the foot and preventing it from hanging loose. The peroneal nerves may be exposed to prolonged pressure when the squatting position is used during delivery, and women who use this position must rise and move about whenever possible, to prevent nerve injury.

Another common cause of knee pain is a disorder of the kneecap (patella) that afflicts many women and is exacerbated during pregnancy. The disorder, known as chondromalacia of the patella, is characterized by an ache about the front part of the knee that gets worse with bending and extension of the joint and during prolonged sitting. Patients often complain of discomfort while sitting in a theater with their knees flexed. Predisposing factors to the condition include loose ligaments and a wide pelvis, both of which contribute to the sideways movement of the cap while the knee is being flexed. During pregnancy, symptoms often become more severe due to swelling around the knee, increased workload on the joint, and increased laxity of the ligaments.

Treatment for chondromalacia involves strengthening the muscles around the knee, which can be achieved by performing straight leg lifts and quad-strengthening exercises (see Chapter 7). In addition, ice packs placed on the front of the knee two to three times a day may help reduce the symptoms. A restraining brace preventing the sideways motion of the kneecap may also be helpful. If these measures fail, one or two injections of a steroid anti-inflammatory preparation immediately beneath the kneecap can dramatically alleviate the pain.

If chondromalacia of the patella first appeared during pregnancy, symptoms disappear after delivery in the majority of cases. The problem may reappear once the child begins to crawl, forcing the mother to squat and kneel.

■ Hip Pain

Hip pain in pregnant women is often associated with low back pain that radiates to the pelvic area through the sciatic nerve. However, if no low backache is present, symptoms in the hip may be caused by erosion in the femoral head, the cap of the thigh bone. Tissues in the femoral head may start to die due to alcoholism, trauma, chronic use of steroids, and certain diseases, such as Cushing's syndrome, but the process may also be triggered by pregnancy.

Recent studies suggest that during pregnancy, tissue erosion in the hip joint may be caused by high levels of hormones combined with increased workload on the bones. Symptoms can be relieved by using a walker or crutches to reduce the stress on the hip. Some doctors advise wearing a special binder or orthopedic girdle to alleviate the hip separation. If the pain persists after delivery, the woman should consult a physician for an orthopedic evaluation.

■ Pubic Pain

As the ligaments of the pelvis loosen in preparation for delivery, bones that are usually joined in a fixed position separate by three to seven millimeters and become mobile. Increased motion in symphysis pubis, the bony mass bounding the front of the pelvis, can lead to irritation and tenderness or pain in the pubic area. The pain generally gets worse with exercise, straining, or walking up the stairs. In mild cases it can be treated by bed rest and application of ice packs.

In contrast to the partial separation of the bones, complete dislocation may occur at the time of delivery. This condition, which occurs very seldom, is successfully treated by bed rest and placing the patient in pelvic girdles.

In rare instances pubic pain is a sign of osteitis pubis, a painful condition characterized by bone erosion in the front of the pelvis. It may be a result of surgical trauma, but also occurs during pregnancy. Typically the pain appears gradually and becomes excruciating over a few days, radiating to the thighs. It is aggravated by any movement of the legs, especially those that stretch the inner thigh muscles. The pain is intense for several days or weeks, then subsides gradually as the bones reossify, restoring the architecture of the pelvis.

Osteitis pubis is often disabling and requires prolonged bed rest. To alleviate discomfort, the woman should seek a position in which her hips are flexed and the legs closed together and pulled in (adduction). Pain may be relieved by ice bags, but injection of a local anesthetic may sometimes be necessary.

■ *Leg Cramps*

Pregnant women commonly complain of cramps in the legs that are often particularly bothersome at night. If the cramps occur frequently calcium tablets may be recommended. Although supplemental calcium can be purchased over the counter, it should be taken only upon a physician's prescription, just like any other medication during pregnancy. To alleviate occasional cramps it may be helpful to stretch the leg and "point" the heel, or to stand up, putting all the weight on the affected leg. Cool-down exercises after each workout can also help prevent leg cramps.

Late in pregnancy, leg cramps may be due to compression of nerves by the enlarged uterus. In this case a change of position, particularly drawing the legs to the chest, may provide a remedy. Wearing support stockings may also help.

■ Round-ligament Pains

The round ligaments are straps of tissue that hold the uterus in place. As the uterus grows larger and heavier they stretch and may occasionally cause spasms of pain on one or both sides of the abdomen and toward the groin area. Although the pain, which is typically sharp and stabbing, can be a frightening experience for the woman, it is in fact quite common in pregnancy and is no cause for concern. The cramps may sometimes be relieved by simply changing position, especially pulling in the knees to adopt a "fetal" posture. If the cramps persist, massage of the area and application of heat may be helpful.

■ Sciatic Pain

Sciatic pain occurs when the fetus exerts pressure on blood vessels and tissues that in turn compress the sciatic nerve, which runs from the buttocks down the back of both legs. The pain is a sharp, piercing sensation that is especially acute in the pelvic area but can be felt along the entire leg. It can be relieved by taking a warm (not hot) shower, applying a hot water bottle or heating pad, or changing the position of the legs, particularly pulling the knees toward the chest.

■ Back Pain

Back pain is extremely common in the general population. Up to seventy-five percent of people will need medical attention for significant aches in the back at some point in their lives. Back pain is also a very common complaint in pregnancy: It is experienced by approximately half of pregnant women. The incidence increases with age and with the number of children the woman has had. If backaches were present before pregnancy they are liable to get worse as the pregnancy develops.

During pregnancy, aches in the back can be due to mechanical factors, such as the increase in body weight and its uneven distribution and changes in the musculoskeletal system triggered by hormonal activity.

Pain in the upper part of the back may be caused by the strain on the muscles supporting the weight of the enlarged breasts. Stooping, wearing high heels, and poor posture can aggravate the stress on the muscles and contribute to the pain. A good support bra and adopting a proper posture while standing and walking can often relieve a high backache.

To check your posture, stand with your back against a wall with feet flat on the floor and heels three to four inches from the wall. Press your shoulders and buttocks to the wall, then try to walk in this position, keeping the spine as straight as possible.

Even more common during pregnancy is pain in the lower back. It may radiate to one or both buttocks and is often persistent albeit not severe. The pain usually gets worse with walking and better with rest (see Fig. 7).

One of the major causes of low back pain is looseness of ligaments brought about by pregnancy hormones. The laxity of the pelvic joints places additional strain on the ligaments at the site of their attachment to pelvic bones, often resulting in pain. Looseness of ligaments in the foot area affects posture adjustment, also contributing to pain in the lower back. Posture adjustment is another significant factor contributing to low backache. To compensate for the growing weight of the uterus, the woman tends to throw her shoulders back, while her pelvis is tilted forward.

To minimize injury, women must learn preferred methods of posture adjustment and lifting techniques. For example, a heavy object must be held close to the body while being lifted, to reduce the forces acting on the lower back.

In addition to maintaining proper posture, pain in the lower back can be reduced by strengthening the muscles of the back, the abdominals, and the muscles attached to the spine and pelvis. During advanced stages of pregnancy the abdominal muscles are lengthened and are less effective in reducing the forward tilt of the pelvis. At this time low back pain caused by the tilt of the pelvis can be relieved by increasing the strength of the hamstring muscles in the legs. Wearing a supportive belt can reduce mobility in the pelvic joint, but it may lead to atrophy of the muscles responsible for pelvic stability and should therefore be accompanied by exercise aimed at strengthening these muscles. Using a firm

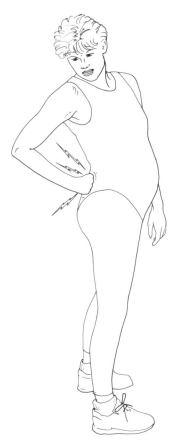

Fig. 7. Lower back pain is one of the most common orthopedic problems encountered during pregnancy.

▪ **CASE STUDY**

Alicia, a thirty-six-year-old word processor, was in the third trimester of her third pregnancy when she began to experience daily backaches. Although working and managing a household kept Alicia very busy, she led a rather sedentary life when it came to physical activity. This lack of exercise was the major source of her lower back pain.

During one of her routine checkups Alicia asked her obstetrician if there were exercises she could do to lessen her back pain. "It may be a bit late to start an exercise program," she commented, "but I still have two months to go and my backache seems to get worse by the day!"

Her doctor assured her that it's never too late to begin exercising, so long as moderation and common sense prevail. He found that her abdominal muscles were very thinned out, allowing her abdomen to protrude even more than is usually the case during her stage of pregnancy. He prescribed a mild exercise program to strengthen her back and abdominal muscles. He also recommended that she wear a supportive abdominal binding to ease the burden on her weakened abdominal muscles.

Following delivery Alicia was advised to begin the exercises outlined in Chapter 12, "Getting Back in Shape." She also started daily walks, using them as an opportunity both to spend time with her children and enjoy being outdoors.

back support while sitting or driving for long periods of time is also recommended. A bed board or a very firm mattress may be necessary if pain is persistent.

▪ *Osteitis Condensans Ilii*

Osteitis condensans ilii is a thickening in the area of the ilium, the upper part of the bone forming the front walls and sides of the pelvic cavity. It is not known what causes this condition, but during pregnancy it may arise in response to the softening of the ligaments and the additional strain on the pelvis. Symptoms include persistent low back pain that starts in the final trimester of pregnancy or immediately after delivery. Treatment includes posture exercises, strengthening of the abdominal muscles, using a firm mattress or bed board, and wearing a special corset.

Connective-tissue Diseases

■ Rheumatoid Arthritis

Rheumatoid arthritis is an inflammation of the lining of the joints, triggered by an autoimmune process in which the immune system mounts an attack against healthy tissue. Symptoms include stiffness, pain, and tenderness in the joint, swelling, and fever. It is not known what causes the condition, although there is some evidence that an infection may be at fault. This type of arthritis often affects young people and can sometimes be crippling.

Patients with rheumatoid arthritis typically go through ups and downs, and pregnancy often brings about an improvement. Some experts have suggested that increased levels of the hormone cortisol in the blood during pregnancy may be responsible for the temporary remissions, but the evidence to this effect is not clear-cut and the precise reason for the improvement remains unknown.

Remissions occur in approximately seventy percent of pregnant woman suffering from rheumatoid arthritis. They tend to begin in the first trimester and persist for the remainder of the pregnancy. In the vast majority of women, however, symptoms recur within two months of delivery.

■ *Lupus*

Systemic lupus erythematosus is also an autoimmune disease, which primarily affects women of childbearing age. Its symptoms include pain and inflammation of the joints, inflammation of the heart membrane (pericarditis), kidney disease, anemia, neurological problems, and personality changes.

Pregnancy in lupus patients is controversial because it can aggravate the condition, particularly if active kidney disease is present. In addition, there is a risk that medications taken against symptoms of lupus may lead to birth defects.

Most physicians believe that lupus patients with active kidney disease or a serious central nervous system disorder should not become pregnant. If, on the other hand, their illness has been under control with relatively small amounts of medication and they are willing to accept the risks associated with pregnancy, they are not advised against it.

Patients who receive antimalarial drugs or immunosuppressive therapy are advised not to have babies because of the risk of birth defects associated with these medications. If they do become pregnant they must be closely monitored and undergo regular tests.

10

WORK AND PREGNANCY

Just how safe is it for a woman to continue working during pregnancy? It seems a bit illogical that we should be addressing this question in the 1990s, when the large majority of women work both in and out of the home. And during pregnancy at least fifty percent of women continue to work outside the home at least part of the time. Still, in this era of increasing litigation, a growing number of employers are considering whether they may be liable for any job-related harm to either a pregnant woman or her baby.

The legal issues still are not fully resolved, even though the Supreme Court recently ruled that women of reproductive age could not be barred from working with materials that may be hazardous to a fetus. That ruling, which involved the manufacturing of batteries, overturned a company rule that had banned women from handling certain materials on the basis that exposure to the materials carried a risk of birth defects.

Women's groups oppose such bans because they fear they will pave the way for other companies to exclude women from high-paying jobs that involve physical labor or other potential hazards to pregnancy.

The published scientific literature provides conflicting reports as to whether work per se is a cause for birth defects or other adverse outcomes of pregnancy. One confounding element is that, although working women generally have favorable demographic and behavioral charcteristics, their reproductive histories tend to be less favorable than those of nonworking women. Unfortunately, few scientific studies have considered the effects of various types of work on the developing baby or the health of the mother. Indeed, the entire issue is one surrounded by controversy, litigation, and speculation. Since there are only limited scientific data, based mostly on epidemiological studies, to support or refute claims, any advice we can offer must be couched in general terms. As discussed in previous chapters, it has long been known that hard physical labor and/or intensive exercise increases the likelihood of having an undersized baby. They may also result in prematurity or pregnancy loss. But questions such as "How much work is safe?" or "At what point should a woman stop working?" have not been assessed in scientific, controlled studies.

Table 10:1 WORK DURING PREGNANCY

Concerns:

- Stress (psychological vulnerability)
- Nonsupportive work environment
- Possible environmental hazards (for example, pesticides, radiation exposure, etc.)

Benefits:

- Financial resources
- Insurance and other health resources
- Professional satisfaction

In trying to determine whether a particular job or workplace is potentially hazardous to a pregnant woman or her baby, a number of factors should be evaluated (see Table 10:1).

■ Stress

In evaluating stress it is important to note that it may be positive or negative. For example, a job that has frequent deadlines may entail considerable stress. To some this stress may be worrisome and negative. If, however, you are a person who enjoys working under pressure and finds meeting deadlines challenging and rewarding, the stress may be positive. Although many accounts of both beneficial and harmful effects of stress appear in the popular media, there is little scientific evidence to support these claims. In general, it has been observed that women who are under a good deal of negative stress have an increased incidence of small birth weight babies and premature labor. For example, epidemiological studies of women obstetricians have found that they have a higher than average incidence of miscarriages, prematurity, and small babies. But whether this is due to increased stress or to other factors, such as poor eating habits, is open to speculation. It is possible that increased levels of stress hormones may in some way trigger premature labor, but more study is needed to document this.

■ Nonsupportive Work Environment

Many jobs, including housework and caring for a young child, entail lifting and/or strenuous labor. The hazards of such activities are similar to those described earlier in the discussion of weight lifting and very vigorous exercise. Such activities carry a risk of orthopedic injury as well as possible impaired blood flow to the uterus. Numerous epidemiological studies show that women who continue to work at such jobs until near the end of pregnancy have smaller than average babies.

For example, a study of French factory workers found that women who began their maternity leaves early had a sixty percent lower incidence of premature deliveries (less than thirty-seven weeks gestation) than women who worked through the pregnancy. Thus, women whose jobs demand strenuous labor may want to consider an early maternity leave to allow them to increase their periods of rest during the final month or so of pregnancy.

■ *Restrictive Work Positions (Prolonged Sitting, Standing, or Inability to Change Position)*

Of all the possible job-related risk factors, this is one of the most common and perhaps most detrimental. A number of epidemiologic studies have documented that women whose jobs demand prolonged periods of standing in one place have an increased incidence of under-sized babies or premature labor. This is probably due to the reduced cardiac output associated with this position. Dizziness or even fainting

Table 10:2 EFFECTS OF WORK DURING PREGNANCY

Work Position	Anatomical/Physiological Change	Potential Effects
Standing	Swayback (lordosis) Reduced cardiac output	Low-back pain Dizziness Premature labor Small babies
Sitting	Swayback (lordosis) Relaxed (dilated) veins	Low-back pain Varicose veins Hemorrhoids
	Compression of abdominal blood vessels	Swollen feet and legs (pedal edema)
Lifting	Swayback (lordosis) Rounded upper back (kyphosis)	Low-back pain
	Straining (Valsalva maneuver)	Premature labor Small babies

may occur when changing positions abruptly, such as standing up after a period of sitting or lying down. (This is called orthostatic hypotension.) The prolonged standing or sitting may also exacerbate varicose veins in susceptible women.

Prolonged sitting, although not as potentially hazardous as standing, may produce adverse effects, particularly backaches. Working at a computer terminal or typing may increase the risk of carpal tunnel syndrome (repetitive-stress syndrome). Sitting for long periods may also worsen hemorrhoids (see Table 10:2).

▪ Environmental Hazards

Many jobs, including working in the home, may involve exposure to pesticides and other chemicals. Some studies have found an increased incidence of birth defects among migrant workers who are exposed to pesticides. It should be noted that similar pesticides are sometimes used in homes and backyard gardens. Certain cleaning substances used both industrially and at home may be hazardous, and a pregnant woman may want to avoid their use.

Exposure to secondhand tobacco smoke may have a detrimental effect on both the mother and fetus, but evidence for this is mostly from epidemiological (population) studies.

The issue of indoor pollution has gained considerable media attention recently. For example, air-quality studies of work environments in buildings built over parking garages or highways have found that indoor pollution actually exceeds outdoor pollution. If you fear that your work environment is hazardous, contact your local Environmental Protection Agency or Occupational Safety and Health Administration.

11

NUTRITIONAL NEEDS
OF THE ACTIVE
PREGNANT WOMAN

Proper nutrition is always important, but during pregnancy it is especially critical. A well-balanced diet will help you to cope more effectively with the caloric cost of pregnancy and the postpartum period, avoiding malnutriton-related complications. What you eat could determine the health and well-being of your baby, since your diet is now supplying essential nutrients to you and your developing child.

Numerous studies show that malnourished mothers are much more likely than their well-nourished counterparts to deliver low birth weight babies. These smaller-than-normal infants not only have a higher risk of serious problems, including death in the neonatal period, but they also are more likely to suffer a variety of health problems throughout life. Low birth weight babies often fail to thrive during the first few weeks of life and they have an increased risk of sudden infant death syndrome (SIDS, or "crib death" as it is commonly called). They are also more likely to have such physical handicaps as hearing and visual disorders, lower IQs, mental retardation, hyperactivity, and other health problems.

Experience underscores the dramatic effect maternal diet has on fetal growth. For example, when in 1944–45 a twenty-eight-week food embargo in western Holland resulted in the average daily food ration being cut from 1,800 to 600 calories per day, women in their last two trimesters of pregnancy had babies whose birth weights were nine percent lower than babies born before the food shortage. There was also an increased incidence of stillbirths as well as infant deaths during the first six weeks of life.

In the United States a study done at the Harvard School of Public Health showed that ninety-five percent of mothers who ate well-balanced diets had healthy babies, and only five percent had babies in fair or poor health. Of those women who ate nutritionally poor diets, only eight percent had healthy babies. An astounding two out of three had babies with serious problems, include late fetal death, prematurity, and a variety of congenital defects.

Although all pregnant women need proper nutrition, the amounts of nutrients they require may vary slightly from woman to woman. The metabolic changes of pregnancy, including the body's greater efficiency in using the nutrients it receives, make it difficult to offer a precise nutrition prescription that applies to all women. For example, a woman who is underweight going into pregnancy may need to gain more than normal-weight women, whereas overweight women may need to gain slightly less. Diets should not be attempted in pregnancy, since they may have a deleterious effect on the offspring. Women who are physically active require more calories than their sedentary counterparts because they need extra energy for their own needs in addition to meeting the requirements of pregnancy. But before discussing the specific nutritional requirements for both sedentary and active pregnant women, it is important to understand more about nutrition and weight gain for pregnancy in general.

■ *Proper Weight Gain*

We've all heard the old saying that when you're pregnant you are eating for two. Actually, that's true, but this does not mean that you need to eat twice as much as you normally do. Remember, one of the "two" you are eating for is a tiny, developing fetus whose caloric requirements are much lower than your own. Eating as much of whatever you want and gaining too much weight is not in the best interest of you or your fetus. In general, you need to consume an extra three hundred calories a day—and proportionately more if you are active.

Good nutrition for a healthy pregnancy includes a well-balanced diet that will allow you to gain an appropriate amount of weight. The consensus among medical professionals is that a woman who was at her desired weight before becoming pregnant should gain between twenty-two and twenty-eight pounds during pregnancy. A recent report from the National Institutes of Health recommended a minimum weight gain of twenty-five pounds for normal-weight, moderately active women. Underweight women should gain between twenty-six and thirty pounds. Obese women, who are twenty percent above the standard weight for their height, should strive for a gradual, progressive weight gain of twenty to twenty-two pounds. (We do not recommend dieting and weight loss during pregnancy; instead, following weaning from breast-feeding, overweight women should engage in a gradual weight-loss program based on a moderate reduction in caloric intake and increased exercise.) In general, you can expect to gain about three to four pounds during the first three months of pregnancy, and that same amount per month during the rest of your pregnancy.

Only a couple of decades ago women were cautioned to limit their weight gain to twelve or fifteen pounds. We now know that this is not enough, and the recommended gain has been revised upward. Still, many women cling to the old notion that it is hard to lose the weight gained during pregnancy, and some weight-conscious women persist in shortchanging themselves and their babies as far as food intake is concerned. Understandably, active, weight-conscious women may become concerned at the prospect of gaining twenty-five or thirty pounds. Remember, though, that this extra weight, gained through a sound, well-balanced diet, will be lost at delivery, being by and large the weight of the products of conception. It may also help you to understand just how the weight is distributed throughout your pregnancy and why good nutrition is so important.

Consider first that you need enough nutrients to support the growth of an average seven-and-one-half-pound baby. Four pounds is the additional maternal blood volume plus another two-and-one-half pounds of tissue and muscle to enlarge and support the uterus. A mother's breasts account for another three pounds, while amniotic fluid weighs two pounds, and the placenta one pound. To ensure that you have enough calories for breast-feeding, you need to gain only five pounds of fat (see Table 11:2). The daily cost of breast-feeding is approximately five hundred calories.

As we stated earlier, in order to gain the proper amount of weight, women who engage in a very rigorous exercise program—defined as a minimum of thirty minutes of high intensity exercise each day—have greater and different nutritional needs during pregnancy than women who follow a more moderate regimen, such as twenty minutes of exercise three or four times a week.

■ Nutritional Requirements of Active Women

Obtaining adequate amounts of calories, protein, and other nutrients is essential to achieve and maintain a healthy pregnancy. Generally, this means daily servings of a variety of foods from the four basic food groups: protein foods (meat, eggs, fish, legumes), milk and dairy products, grains and cereals, and fruits and vegetables (see Table 11:1). Remember, however, that there are many acceptable ways of providing the nutrients necessary for good fetal growth. What is most important is consuming a wide variety of nutritious foods that will provide sufficient calories and nutrients for an optimal pregnancy.

■ Calories

A typical pregnancy requires a total of about eighty thousand additional calories. That may seem like a great deal, but spread out over the nine months of pregnancy it only amounts to approximately three hundred extra calories per day above what you would normally consume when not pregnant. About a third of these calories are used in maternal fat gain, but the remainder provide the energy needed for the fetus, metabolic changes, and to provide for new blood and other tissue needed by the mother. When pregnant, then, you need to choose your foods wisely. A three-hundred-calorie brownie would meet your added calorie requirements, but such "empty calories" would not provide you with necessary nutrients. On the other hand, such "nutrient-dense" foods as a pint of low-fat milk or a tuna or chicken sandwich on whole-grain bread would provide the necessary extra three hundred calories as well as critical minerals, vitamins, and proteins.

It is important, therefore, to avoid the empty calories of sugar- and fat-rich foods, for they provide little nutritional value. Instead, choose such nutrient-rich foods as skim milk, cottage cheese, fish, lean meats, eggs, fruits, and leafy dark-green vegetables, all of which provide important vitamins and minerals to help the fetus develop normally.

Furthermore, because most of the fetus's growth occurs in the last trimester, it is essential to maintain your additional calorie intake during the last three months of your pregnancy. Even if you think you've gained enough weight, never attempt to cut calories during this critical period.

■ Protein

In 1989 the Food and Nutrition Board of the National Research Council revised its Recommended Dietary Allowances (RDA), which now call for pregnant women to consume sixty grams of protein a day, only slightly more than the forty-five to fifty grams recommended for a nonpregnant woman nineteen to fifty years of age (see Table 11:3). Since many American women already eat more than this amount, there is usually no reason to greatly increase protein intake during pregnancy. Eating high-protein breads and cereals, an additional serving of lean meat, fish, or chicken, or drinking one or two extra glasses of milk a day is generally all you will need to get sufficient protein. Nonetheless, we recommend that pregnant women monitor their protein intake to ensure that they're getting enough, especially if they follow a vegetarian diet or eat very little meat or other animal products.

■ *Vitamin A*

Vitamin A is one of the fat-soluble vitamins that can be stored in the body. The RDA for vitamin A is eight hundred retinol equivalents (RE), the same as before pregnancy. Adequate vitamin A is needed for the proper formation of skin and the linings of ducts in the gastrointestinal, urinary, and respiratory tracts of the fetus. Deficiencies of vitamin A can cause abnormalities and impaired vision in some children. We recommend this RDA be met through dietary sources rather than supplements. Good sources of vitamin A include liver, dark-green or dark-yellow vegetables and fruits, whole milk, eggs, and fortified margarine. Don't overdo it by taking over-the-counter vitamins. High-dose vitamin A supplements during pregnancy may cause severe birth defects. It is almost impossible to consume dangerous amounts of vitamin A from the diet alone, but as little as five to ten times the RDA—the amount in some megadose vitamin A pills—can cause birth defects. You also should avoid isotretinoin (Accutane), an acne medicine that is made from a derivative of vitamin A. Since vitamin A is stored in the body you should discontinue Accutane (or high-dose supplements) before becoming pregnant.

■ *Thiamine, Riboflavin, and Niacin*

These are important B vitamins that are needed for a variety of metabolic functions. Without adequate amounts of these vitamins the body cannot properly utilize carbohydrates, protein, or fats. Niacin also is essential to form the fetus's nervous system.

The RDA for pregnant women calls for 17 milligrams of niacin a day, 1.6 milligrams of riboflavin, and 1.5 milligrams of thiamine—in each instance, slightly more than before pregnancy. These RDAs can be met easily be eating a variety of foods. Specifically, high amounts of thiamine are found in pork, beef, nuts, whole grains, and wheat germ. Milk, cheese, meats, wheat germ, and leafy green vegetables contain large amounts of riboflavin. Most foods contain niacin, but fish, meats, peanuts, and whole grains are particularly rich sources. Also, the body can manufacture niacin from the amino acid tryptophan, which is found in high quality (complete) protein.

■ *Vitamins B_6 and B_{12}*

The RDA calls for pregnant women to have 2.2 milligrams of vitamin B_6, compared to 1.6 milligrams before pregnancy. Vitamin B_6 is instrumental in the metabolism of protein and fat. B_6 is widely available in such food as meats, poultry, fish, whole-grain cereals, nuts, seeds, peanut butter, green leafy vegetables, carrots, potatoes, and avocados.

Vitamin B_{12} is needed to build nucleic acid, an essential component of genetic material. It is also needed for the production of red blood cells, and small amounts are essential for the normal functioning of all body cells. Since vitamin B_{12} is found in all foods of animal origin, it is easy to consume the 2.2 milligrams called for by the RDA, and deficiencies are rare. Sometimes, however, strict vegetarians—women who eat no meat, egg, or dairy products—may suffer from B_{12} deficiency. In that case, physician-prescribed supplements should be added to the diet.

■ *Folate (Folic Acid)*

Folate is essential to build red blood cells and the genetic materials in the cell nucleus. Recent studies have found that women who take folate supplements before pregnancy and during the first trimester have a significantly reduced incidence of neural-tube defects, such as spina bifida—a disorder in which the spinal column fails to form normally. Thus, pregnant women should consume a daily total of about four hundred micrograms of folic acid, either by taking physician-prescribed supplements or by eating such folate-rich foods as eggs, leafy vegetables, oranges, legumes, whole-grain cereals, bran, and wheat germ. Twin pregnancy requires a supplement of one milligram per day.

■ *Vitamin C*

Drinking an eight-ounce glass of orange juice can easily provide the total RDA of seventy milligrams of vitamin C (an increase of only ten milligrams) for pregnant women. While it is important for pregnant women to get enough vitamin C, however, we recommend that they do not consume too much. Excessive consumption of vitamin C can condition the fetus to having large amounts of vitamin C in its blood and cause problems after birth when the more normal amounts in breast milk or infant formula are consumed. Also, large doses of vitamin C during pregnancy may promote urinary-tract irritation, bladder stones, and diarrhea.

■ *Vitamin E*

Since the RDA of vitamin E for pregnant women is only two milligrams more per day (or a total of ten milligrams) than for nonpregnant women, it can be satisfied by ordinary consumption of vegetable oil, nuts, seeds, and whole grains.

■ *Calcium, Phosphorus, and Vitamin D*

Pregnant women should increase their calcium and phosphorus intake by fifty percent so that they consume a total of 1,200 mg of each per day. Since vitamin D is essential for proper calcium metabolism, they should also make certain they get ten micrograms of it per day.

Calcium, essential for the formation of the baby's bones and teeth as well as for proper functioning of the blood, nerves, and muscles, is essential during the last three months of pregnancy. During that time the fetus may take as much as thirteen milligrams of calcium each hour from the mother's blood. But mothers are not advised to postpone increasing their calcium intake until the last trimester, because a woman's body stores calcium throughout pregnancy in preparation for the later demands.

The best way for pregnant women to satisfy their calcium requirements is to drink low-fat milk or eat more dairy products, including yogurt and cheese (low fat if you're concerned about calories). Sardines, mackerel, and salmon (if eaten with the bones) and soya milk are other good sources of absorbable calcium (absorbed well by the mother and thus readily available to the fetus). Some dark-green vegetables, such as broccoli, also contain fair amounts of calcium, as do dates, almonds, dried peas, and citrus fruits.

Phosphorus is widely available in many foods, including meats, snack foods, and soft drinks made with phosphates. The intake of phosphorus should be about equal to that of calcium. But since phosphorus is so prevalent some women may consume much more of it than calcium. However, if vitamin D levels, essential for calcium absorption and balance, are adequate, then a high amount of phosphorus should not be harmful. Vitamin D requirements can be met without too much difficulty, since it is manufactured in fatty tissue just under skin that is exposed to sunlight. It is also added to fortified milk. To ensure sufficient levels of vitamin D some doctors prescribe ten micrograms (400 I.U.) per day throughout pregnancy, but we do not recommend this since vitamin D is stored in the body and excessive amounts can be harmful.

■ *Iron*

Pregnant women need as much as twenty milligrams per day (thirty milligrams total) of additional iron in order to produce hemoglobin— the blood pigment that carries oxygen—for the mother's expanded blood supply and to support the placenta. Iron supply is most essential in the last trimester, when the fetus builds up the iron stores it needs during the first six months of life. Breast milk contains very little iron; thus, the fetus should be born with an adequate reserve to last until solid foods are introduced into the baby's diet.

The importance of the additional iron cannot be understated, since inadequate iron causes a deficiency of hemoglobin, which carries oxygen to the cells of the mother's body and oxygen crosses the placenta to the fetus. When there is an iron deficiency the mother's heart must work harder to meet this need, which can lead to excessive fatigue and physiological stress. Severe hemoglobin deficiency even places the mother at risk for cardiac problems. Furthermore, hemorrhaging during the baby's birth can be life-threatening.

Since it is difficult to meet the necessary iron requirements through a normal diet, most physicians prescribe an iron supplement of between 320 and 960 milligrams per day for their pregnant patients. Women who had iron deficiencies before becoming pregnant may receive larger doses. Physicians recommend taking an iron supplement with a citrus juice, since the acids in the juice enhance iron absorption. The downside, however, is that the greater absorbability of inorganic iron can upset the stomach. Never take iron with milk or milk products; they prevent iron from being absorbed by the body.

■ *Iodine*

According to the 1989 RDA, a pregnant woman should have 175 micrograms of iodine daily. An iodine deficiency could lead to a deficiency in thyroid hormone, which in turn can cause cretinism, a condition characterized by greatly impaired mental and physical ability and facial features similar to those of Down syndrome. Too much iodine could lead to infant goiter (enlargement of the thyroid gland) and hypothyroidism, as well as mental retardation. In some instances the infant may die.

Iodine deficiency is now rare, thanks to the wide availability of foods grown in iodine-rich soil. At one time, there were so-called goiter belts in the Midwest and certain mountainous regions where people ate mostly local produce. This problem has been resolved by adding iodine to salt. Thus, normal use of iodized salt and a diet that includes seafood and other foods grown in the coastal regions of the U.S. where iodine is found in the soil will provide adequate amounts.

■ Zinc

Since zinc is critical to proper cell growth of the fetus, the RDA calls for pregnant women's diets to include three extra milligrams of zinc, for a total of fifteen milligrams. Studies suggest that too little zinc in the mother's diet might lead to hypertension, abnormal deliveries, nervous-system malformations, and lower birth weight babies. But again, a balance is needed. Megadoses of zinc during pregnancy have been linked to premature births, stillbirths, and birth deformities. High-zinc foods include meat, poultry, seafood (especially oysters), spinach, dairy products, egg yolks, dry peas and beans, nuts, and wheat germ.

■ Copper

Copper is found in abundance in vegetables. Low copper levels have been linked to premature labor.

▪ *Sodium*

In the past, health-care professionals encouraged pregnant women to avoid salt because they believed high sodium intake caused hypertension (toxemia). More recent research reveals that restricting sodium consumption does not prevent hypertension; thus, the salt ban has been lifted. Yet we do not condone a high-salt diet, which can lead to fluid retention and hypertension in some women. Processed foods are already so highly seasoned that further salting is not needed or recommended, but pregnant women can salt natural foods to taste.

▪ *Special Advice for Pregnant Vegetarians*

Pregnant women who are partial vegetarians and merely avoid red meat and women who avoid all meat, poultry, and fish but eat dairy products and eggs should have no problem in meeting the RDAs for pregnant women through their normal diets. The only exception might be iron, but even nonvegetarians usually need to take an iron supplement.

Vegetarians who avoid *all* meat, egg, and milk products are at risk for deficiencies of riboflavin, vitamin B_{12}, calcium, zinc, and iron. They must be careful, therefore, to eat a wide variety of vegetables, legumes, and nuts in combination with grains to consume enough protein to satisfy the amino acid requirements of mother and fetus. If, however, protein consumption is still inadequate we recommend that these women supplement their diets with milk and eggs, as well as an iron supplement, during pregnancy and breast-feeding.

▪ *Nutritional Recommendations for Active Pregnant Women*

The specific needs of highly active pregnant women have not been studied formally. However, since much is understood about the nutritional needs of pregnancy and the nutritional requirements for women engaged in heavy physical activity, we can make the following general recommendations.

Increased caloric intake. Since the energy required for physical activities is greater late in pregnancy than in the early or middle stages, highly active pregnant women need more than three hundred additional calories per day. Although the energy needs of women will vary with the amount and type of activity they engage in, we recommend five hundred additional calories for women who are maintaining a thirty-minute daily exercise program during pregnancy. More calories may be required by women who exercise more.

A good way to tell if you are consuming enough calories is to monitor your weight. If the rate of weight gain begins to fall below normal at any point, you will need to consume additional calories.

We recommend that physically active women eat to appetite, since most people have the ability to adjust energy intake to meet their body's demands. Furthermore, we recommend a diet high in complex carbohydrates because carbohydrates best replace muscle glycogen (stored glucose) lost during exercise.

Base protein intake on energy expended. Since most Americans normally eat more than enough protein, you probably already consume sufficient amounts to compensate for the additional demands of pregnancy and exercise. A diet in which twelve percent of the energy consumed is protein should be adequate. To be sure you're getting enough, however, base the amount of protein you consume on the number of calories you burn off. For example, an active pregnant woman consuming 2,300 calories per day should ingest 69 grams of protein daily, but a woman who needs to consume 3,000 calories per day should increase her protein intake to 90 grams.

Maintain iron consumption. Both physically active and more sedentary pregnant women need to consume the same amount of iron during their pregnancy—about thirty milligrams a day. As noted earlier, we recommend that pregnant patients ensure their iron intake through consumption of an iron supplement.

Women who begin a training program after they become pregnant may have greater needs since additional iron is required for the blood volume expansion associated with pregnancy. We do not, however, recommend initiating any rigorous exercise program once pregnancy is begun.

Drink more water. Part and parcel of a healthy pregnancy is the expansion of total body water. Most likely, the physically active pregnant woman needs to consume even more water to support expansion of total body water and to maintain normal body temperature. Therefore, we recommend drinking eight to twelve cups of water daily, or one glass of water for each hour of physical activity, to maintain normal hydration and expansion of total body water.

Use salt to taste. If you participate in a rigorous exercise program and if your sodium intake is low, you may be placing yourself at risk for sodium depletion. But since most American women consume at least double the amount of sodium they need anyway, it is highly unlikely that this situation will occur. We recommend, therefore, normal salt-to-taste consumption.

■ *Warnings for All Pregnant Women*

We recommend that all pregnant women heed the following warnings during their pregnancy:

Avoid alcohol. Drinking during pregnancy can result in giving birth to a baby with fetal alcohol syndrome (FAS), a condition in which babies are below normal in weight, height, and head circumference. FAS babies may be deformed and may suffer from mental and physical retardation. Although the amount of alcohol needed to produce FAS is not known, we recommend that pregnant women avoid all alcohol, including that found in food (such as rum-soaked pastries) and drugs (like cough medicine).

Limit caffeine. Although it is difficult to ascertain the effects of caffeine in human beings, there is some evidence to suggest that caffeine may contribute to increasing a pregnant woman's risk of premature birth, stillbirth, and birth defects. We do know that caffeine acts as a diuretic, causing the kidneys to excrete more urine; thus, high caffeine levels in the mother's blood can lead to excessive loss of fluids and nutrients needed by both mother and fetus during the pregnancy. We recommend limiting daily consumption of caffeine to about three hundred milligrams, or the amount in two cups of brewed coffee, which should be consumed throughout the day.

Don't smoke. Studies reveal that women who smoke double their risk for delivery of low birth weight babies and are more likely to have spontaneous abortions, premature deliveries, stillbirths, infant deaths, and complications involving the placenta. For these reasons we recommend that pregnant women do not smoke.

Avoid all illicit drugs and unneeded medications. Since so many drugs can cross the placental barrier and harm the fetus, we recommend limiting medications during pregnancy to those drugs that are essential to the health of the mother or fetus or prescribed by your physician. We urge pregnant women to consult with their physicians before taking any drug, including over-the-counter pain-killers. This recommendation includes over-the-counter medications as well as prescription drugs. Even more important is total abstinence from mind-altering drugs like crack, cocaine, heroin, and marijuana. The growing epidemic of illicit drug use, especially of crack and other forms of cocaine, has resulted in an increasing number of severely ill, addicted babies. There is no such thing as a safe amount of these drugs during pregnancy. The best time to stop their use is well before pregnancy is attempted.

Table 11:1 DAILY FOOD NEEDS

	Group 1 Fruits and vegetables	Group 2 Whole-grain or enriched breads	Group 3 Milk and milk products	Group 4 Meat, poultry, fish, eggs, nuts, and beans
Important functions	Fights off infections; promotes healthy skin and good eyesight	Provides energy and fiber to avoid constipation	Builds bones and teeth; aids growth of new tissue and repair of body cells	Helps build new body tissue; prevents anemia
Nutrients	Minerals Vitamins	Carbohydrates Minerals Vitamins Protein	Calcium Phosphorus Protein Vitamins	Protein Iron Vitamins
Daily Servings	4 or more	4 or more	4 or more	3 or more
Special Considerations	Select one serving rich in vitamin A (dark-yellow or green leafy vegetables—broccoli, spinach, greens, carrots, winter squash) and one serving rich in vitamin C (citrus fruit, tomatoes, or other fruit such as cantaloupe or strawberries)		If you don't like milk, substitute items made from milk, such as yogurt, cottage cheese, or custard	Organ meats, such as liver and kidneys, are particularly good. Be sure to add a little cheese, milk, or meat to meals with main dishes made of dry beans, peas, nuts, lentils, or other legumes

Amount (count as one serving)			
a. 1 cup raw, dark-green leafy vegetables	a. 1 slice bread, biscuit, or roll	a. 8-oz. glass milk, buttermilk, or skim milk	a. 2–3 oz. cooked meat, fish, or poultry
b. ½ cup cooked vegetables or fruit	b. 1 oz. (¾ cup) ready-to-eat cereal	b. 1⅓ cups cottage cheese	b. 1 cup cooked dry beans, peas, or lentils
c. 1 medium-sized fruit, such as an orange, apple, or banana, or ½ grapefruit	c. ½ cup cooked cereal: rice, oatmeal, corn meal, grits, or pasta (macaroni, noodles, spaghetti)	c. 1½ slices (1½ oz.) cheese	c. 4 Tbsp. peanut butter
d. ½ cup fruit juice	d. 2 graham crackers	d. 1½ cups ice cream	d. 2 eggs

Sample Food Plan for One Day

Meals

Group 1 orange juice	Group 1 apple	Group 1 broccoli
2 slices toast	2 ham &	2 rice
3 milk	3 cheese	3 milk
4 two eggs	4 sandwich	4 chicken

Snacks

Group 4 peanut butter	Group 1 carrot sticks	Group 3 ice cream
2 crackers	3 yogurt dip	
3 milk	1 tomato juice	

Source: *Pregnancy and Food.* American College of Obstetricians and Gynecologists (ACOG), Washington, D.C. Reprinted with permission of ACOG.

Table 11:2 WHERE THE WEIGHT GOES

Average Weight Gain in Pregnancy (in Pounds)

The baby	
Fetus	7.5
Placenta	1
Amniotic fluid	2
The mother	
Fat and protein stores	4–6
Increased fluid volume	1–3
Uterus	2.5
Breast enlargement	3
Increased blood volume	4
Total	24 to 28 pounds

Table 11:3 RECOMMENDED DIETARY ALLOWANCES (RDA) DURING PREGNANCY

RDA Nutrients	Regular (add for pregnancy) = total
Protein (gm)*	46–50 (+10–15) = 60
Vitamin A (RE)	800
Vitamin D (mcg)	5–10 (+0–5) = 10
Vitamin E (mg)	8 (+2) = 10
Ascorbic acid (mg)	60 (+10) = 70
Folic acid (folacin) (mcg)	180 (+220) = 400
Niacin (mg)	13–15 (+2–4) = 17
Riboflavin (mg)	1.2–1.3 (+.3–.4) = 1.6
Thiamine (mg)	1.0–1.1 (+.4–.5) = 1.5
Vitamin B_6 (mg)	1.6 (+.6) = 2.2
Vitamin B_{12} (mg)	2.0 (+.2) = 2.2
Calcium (mg)	800–1,200 (+0–400) = 1,200
Phosphorus (mg)	800–1,200 (+0–400) = 1,200
Iodine (mcg)	150 (+25) = 175
Magnesium (mg)	280 (+40) = 320
Zinc (mg)	12 (+3) = 15

From the Food and Nutrition Board, National Academy of Sciences–National Research Council, Washington, D.C., revised 1980.
*Key to abbreviations: gm = gram; RE = retinol equivalents; mcg = microgram; mg = milligram

12

GETTING BACK
IN SHAPE

Most women, regardless of their level of physical activity, want to get back in shape as soon as possible after giving birth. First-time mothers in particular are dismayed to find they can't fit into their prepregnancy clothes even several months after their baby is born. Often they feel tired and less energetic than they did before giving birth. Postpartum depression, often called the "baby blues," is another phenomenon that catches some new mothers unaware.

Exercise is a form of relaxation and, when done regularly, in moderation, and with a strong dose of common sense, aids in relieving many of the stressful symptoms women experience during the postnatal period. Before specifying the do's and don't's of effective postnatal exercise programs, it is best to understand all that is involved in the physical recovery from childbirth.

■ What to Expect After Giving Birth

After spending an often uncomfortable few months in the final stages of pregnancy, most women look forward to the day when they can regain their normal fitness level and get on with the new experience of tending to their newborn infant. They are often surprised, therefore, by the amount of physical discomfort they feel after childbirth, particularly in the first six weeks after delivery. Most of this discomfort is normal though, and new mothers should not be alarmed if they experience minor problems during the postnatal period. These often include:

■ Afterpains

At the time of delivery the uterus weighs approximately two pounds. By your first postpartum checkup, four to six weeks after delivery, it has shrunk to only about two ounces. In part the uterus shrinks because its muscle cells are contracting, and it is this contraction that causes the cramping known as afterpains.

New mothers usually suffer the worst cramps when the baby is nursing, particularly in the first few days after delivery. Nursing stimulates the flow of oxytocin, the hormone that is instrumental in initiating the contractions of labor as well as the release of breast milk. The uterine contractions are important in the early postpartum period because they help stop bleeding from the uterus. This is yet another argument for breast-feeding, at least in the postpartum period. These afterpains normally subside after a few days. If the cramping is severe your doctor may prescribe a pain reliever to ease any discomfort.

■ Fatigue

It took a good deal of energy for your body to undergo the changes necessary to give birth, and it also will take energy for your body to recover from the stress of pregnancy, labor, and delivery. Thus is it natural for new mothers to feel tired during the postpartum period, particularly now that they have a demanding new schedule.

Don't worry if you feel fatigued, or even exhausted, during those first few weeks. You will begin to feel better if you get as much rest as possible, although that's not easy with a new baby around. The best approach is to try to adjust your sleeping schedule to the baby's; take full advantage of the infant's frequent nap times to rest yourself. We recommend you try to get two naps a day for the first two weeks and at least one nap a day for the next two.

Now is not the time to worry about everyday household chores; what's most important is to grab some quick naps or simply rest with your feet up. Try to have another adult around to help you care for your child and the household; if possible, your husband should take time off from his work (as you probably have done from yours) to help with the baby and the house. Other valuable help can come from a relative, friend, hired housekeeper, or your other children.

■ *Vaginal Bleeding and Discharge*

Lochia, the residual blood discharge that comes from the placenta site, is a normal postpartum phenomenon and is not cause for concern. Typically it lasts anywhere from four to eight weeks, gradually tapering off until it stops altogether. You will notice that for the first four or five days the discharge is bright red; later, it will change to a brownish color. For your own comfort, use sanitary napkins, rather than tampons, to absorb the blood. If the lochia smells bad or is accompanied by fever you may have an infection. In that case notify your doctor immediately.

Occasionally, if and when the uterus relaxes and some of the blood vessels that had closed reopen, you may experience a cessation of the lochia after only a week or two, followed by sudden heavy bleeding, which may mean your uterus did not contract well.

Since postpartum blood loss can lead to iron deficiencies, your doctor will probably recommend that you continue taking iron supplements during this time.

Once lochia ends, you may notice a white, sticky vaginal discharge; it is perfectly normal. Too much discharge or a greenish or yellow discharge, however, may signal an infection and warrant a consultation with your doctor.

■ *Hot Flashes, Excessive Sweating*

Hot flashes, often accompanied by heavy sweating, occur when hormone production drops after childbirth. Since night sweating may lead to chills when outside temperatures drop, we recommend putting a clean, dry nightgown nearby when you go to bed at night.

■ *Urinary Problems*

During pregnancy women retain a great deal of fluid. After childbirth their bodies eliminate that fluid through frequent urination. Inflammation of the bladder and urethra, brought about by the pressure placed upon them in childbirth, can cause a burning sensation during urination. To ease any discomfort we recommend drinking lots of water— enough to make your urine nearly colorless.

You may also find that you leak some urine when you exert yourself suddenly. This occurs because the pelvic muscles have been stretched in childbirth. The problem should resolve itself with time; Kegel exercises to strengthen the pelvic area may also help (see "Postpartum Exercises," this chapter).

■ *Discomfort from Episiotomy*

Sometimes, during childbirth, your doctor will perform an episiotomy, an incision made at the perineum to facilitate delivery. The site of the episiotomy will be tender and painful for a few days after childbirth; it takes about a week before the sensitivity subsides. Occasionally, though, the pain gets worse before it gets better, particularly if the new mother is physically active. Sitting in a shallow tub of warm water—wait about two weeks before taking a full-tub bath—as well as taking warm showers can ease the tenderness and aid healing. Pouring a cup of warm water over the site while urinating can help relieve some of the sting.

Some of the pain you feel in this area is caused by reflex tensing of the muscles of the perineum (the region between the vulva and the anus). Placing an ice pack on the area can help decrease swelling during the first twenty-four hours after childbirth. After that, in addition to keeping the area very clean, you should sit sideways on a cushion to avoid putting pressure on the area. If you notice any redness or swelling in the area consult your doctor immediately. It could be a sign of infection.

■ *Hemorrhoids*

The vein enlargement that occurs in pregnancy and increases during the last few months of pregnancy and childbirth can cause hemorrhoids. This ailment is both uncomfortable and relatively common and is not cause for alarm. Usually, hemorrhoids subside in about four or five weeks. If they persist beyond that time notify your doctor, for they may require professional treatment.

In most cases using a cream or suppositories will ease the discomfort. Many women find cotton pads soaked in witch hazel soothing; chilling the pads in the refrigerator can offer extra comfort. Since constipation can aggravate hemorrhoids, a stool softener can also help. Lying down with the legs elevated helps too, since it relieves pressure on dilated veins.

■ *Constipation*

Most new mothers complain of constipation during the postpartum period. Typically, the problem disappears when they follow a high-fiber diet that includes fresh fruit and vegetables and whole-grain products. Adequate water is also important—you should drink at least eight glasses of fluid, preferably water, a day, and more if you are breast-feeding. Walking around as soon as possible after you give birth is also helpful in restoring normal bowel function. You should have your first bowel movement by the third to fifth day after delivery; if not, you may need a stool softener or mild laxative.

■ Hair Loss

Hair normally grows according to different cycles—that is, some hairs grow while others are preparing to be shed. During pregnancy those cycles get out of kilter, and after delivery a greater than normal amount of hair may go into a resting or shedding phase with many young hairs erupting thereafter. Some women even develop bald spots.

To minimize hair loss, avoid using hot curlers, excessive brushing, blow-drying, and the use of hair dyes—all of which promote hair thinning. Consider a shorter style that makes the thinning less notice-able. Even though the hair loss may be troubling, rest assured that for the large majority of women it's a temporary phenomenon. Within nine to twelve months your hair cycles should be back to normal.

■ Sore Breasts

Inadequate letdown of milk or infrequent nursing can cause a milk duct to become plugged. In turn, this can trigger swelling, redness, or a painful lump in the breasts. To relieve the discomfort, gently massage the area or apply warm compresses. Nursing more frequently also can help.

Contact your doctor, however, if any fever or body aches develop; they may be a sign of mastitis, an infection of the breast. A breast infection that goes untreated can abscess and require surgical drainage, but in most cases early treatment can prevent this from occurring.

Remember, too, that breasts become full, engorged, and tender on the third or fourth day after childbirth. This is due both to the start of heavy milk production and increased blood flow to the breast tissue. The problem will probably last for a day or two until milk begins to flow freely. In the meantime, applying heat or cold to the area, whichever feels best for you, can ease the discomfort.

Women who do not plan to breast-feed may find some relief by binding their breasts and applying ice bags to the area. Usually, discomfort begins to subside in about three days.

A complete physical exam at six weeks after the delivery is imperative. By that time most of the breast enlargement of pregnancy will have gone and it will allow the physician to do a thorough checkup.

■ Menstruation

Women who choose not to breast-feed usually begin menstruating again within eight to twelve weeks after delivery. Nursing mothers often find that their menstrual periods do not resume while they are breast-feeding, although some women start menstruating about two months after childbirth anyway. Others do not resume their periods until six or eight months after the baby is weaned. Remember, however, that the lack of periods does not necessarily denote a similar lack of ovulation. Thus, if you want to avoid pregnancy birth control should be used, even if you are breast-feeding. Talk to your doctor about the safest method. When menstruation does begin, it is sometimes heavier, lighter, or more irregular than it was before pregnancy.

It is also common for the first post-childbirth period to be very heavy, since the uterus is sloughing off an unusually thick lining. If, however, you need to use one or more pads per hour for more than six or seven hours, notify your doctor immediately.

■ Recovery from Cesarean Birth

As you would expect, it often takes longer to recover from a cesarean birth than from a vaginal delivery. Women may feel tired, weak, and unwell for several days. For the first twenty-four to forty-eight hours most of these new mothers are fed intravenously and have a catheter to drain their bladder. As gas accumulates in their bowel they may experience some abdominal pain. When they pass gas, signaling that the intestines are becoming active again, the IV will be disconnected and they will be able to eat once more.

We recommend trying to walk around within a day of birth. While it can be painful, walking helps digestive function and also prevents blood clots in the legs. Full recovery may take several weeks, however.

■ *Postpartum Depression*

New mothers do occasionally experience postpartum depression, with symptoms ranging from a mild case of the "baby blues," stemming from the letdown most women feel following the excitement of pregnancy and childbirth, to mood swings, depression, and anxiety. Fatigue, brought on by insufficient and interrupted sleep, and the emotional tension of becoming a new mother can also exacerbate postpartum depression. Only about one in five hundred women experience puerperal psychosis, an extreme form of depression that usually requires hospitalization. These women by and large had preexisting depression and the delivery just precipitated or exacerbated the condition.

For most women the postpartum blues last anywhere from a few days to a few weeks. Plenty of rest, social support from friends and relatives, and taking a little time for yourself—like going for an occasional long walk without your newborn—can help alleviate the baby blues. If, however, you notice that your symptoms linger beyond six weeks—the point at which the body's hormonal balance is restored—consult a health-care professional. If the problem persists, you may need to consult a psychiatrist.

■ *Exercise: Getting Back in Shape*

Exercise can help you get back in physical shape after pregnancy and childbirth. Regular physical activity can lift your spirits, keep you more energized, and tone and strengthen the muscles that will help you regain your normal figure.

The goal of postpartum exercise is to maintain your highest level of fitness consistent with optimum safety. Bear in mind that during pregnancy the body's connective tissue has softened and stretched. Such tissue laxity and joint instability make you more susceptible to injury during the postpartum period. Additionally, changes in the cardiovascular system that occurred during pregnancy—specifically an elevated heart rate and increased cardiac output—persist for approximately four weeks after childbirth. It is important, therefore, to set your target heart rate approximately twenty-five to thirty percent lower than it was before you became pregnant.

The amount of exercise new mothers can tolerate depends in part upon their prepregnancy level of activity and how comfortable they feel during the workout. Highly active women may be able to participate safely in more strenuous exercise than their more sedentary counterparts. An ideal postpartum exercise program offers women a wide variety of exercise choices, from walking, swimming, and stationary cycling to modified dancing and calisthenics. In consultation with their physician, new mothers can choose and develop the exercise regimen that's most effective for them.

■ *Exercise Guidelines*

The American College of Obstetricians and Gynecologists provides usable guidelines for developing a safe home exercise program during the postpartum period.

- *Exercise regularly.* After the first two weeks, exercise for at least ten minutes a day, gradually increasing workout intensity and frequency as the weeks pass. Do not engage in rigorous competitive activities that can overstress the body.

■ *Do not* exercise vigorously in *hot, humid weather or when you have a fever.* Such workouts place you at risk for dehydration and heat stress.

■ *Avoid jerky, bouncy motions.* Perform any exercises on a wood or carpeted surface to alleviate pressure on bones, joints, and ligaments and to reduce chance of injury.

■ *Avoid deep flexing or extending of joints.* Since your connective tissue is still loose such movements can cause serious damage to ligaments and tendons.

■ *Avoid any exercise* that demands *jumping, jarring motions,* or sudden *changes in direction.*

■ *Follow up* any workout sessions with a *cool-down period* of gradually declining activity. Stretch *gently;* overly rigorous stretching increases risk of joint injury.

■ *Measure your heart rate* when you have reached a *peak* level of activity. Target heart rates should be set at twenty-five to thirty percent lower than before pregnancy (see Table 12:1). Use the "talk test" or RPE 12–14 (see pp. 67–68).

■ After working out on the floor, *rise gradually* to avoid *orthostatic hypotension,* a sudden decrease in blood pressure leading to momentary faintness or dizziness. Also, continue some form of leg activity for a brief period.

■ *Drink lots of water* before and after exercise to prevent dehydration. If necessary, interrupt your exercise session to drink water and replenish body liquids.

■ If you have led a sedentary life-style before and during pregnancy, *begin any postpartum activity at low levels of intensity.* Build to a higher level of activity very gradually.

■ *Stop exercising and consult your physician* immediately if any of the following warning signs appear:
—Pain
—Bleeding
—Dizziness
—Shortness of breath

—Palpitations
—Faintness
—Tachycardia (abnormally rapid heart rate)
—Back pain
—Pubic pain
—Difficulty in walking

■ *Postpartum Exercises*

Regular, moderate exercise is the best way to get fit after pregnancy. Even though new mothers may be anxious to regain their prepregnancy bodies, they should proceed carefully and limit physical activity for the first two weeks after delivery. Mothers who have undergone cesarean deliveries should limit physical activity for four to six weeks. We recommend that all new mothers perform the following exercises.

KEGEL VAGINAL-TIGHTENING EXERCISE

To regain strength in the pelvic supporting tissues that have become stretched by the hormonal and physical changes of pregnancy and delivery, new mothers can begin doing the Kegel exercise immediately after giving birth. Try it lying down at first, with the knees up, slightly apart, and bent at a right angle. Later you can do the exercise while sitting or standing.

Simply squeeze the muscles around the urethra and anus as if you were holding back urine and a bowel movement, and hold for a few seconds; then relax. Do at least ten repetitions, five times daily.

LEGS AND FEET

To prevent varicose veins and leg cramps by improving muscle tone and circulation, lie flat in bed, press the backs of the knees down flat, then relax. Do several repetitions. For the feet, flex and stretch the ankles while lying or sitting in bed. Point feet upward, then flex and stretch toes. Circle feet outward, then inward.

ABDOMEN

Lie flat on the floor or other firm surface. While keeping the small of your back pressed against the floor, lift your shoulders upward with the head and neck straight, then relax and lower shoulders to the floor. Exhale slowly while lifting shoulders. Repeat with a slight twist of the shoulders, lifting shoulders to one side, then the other. Do ten repetitions, three times daily.

In the later stages of the postpartum period you can try the donkey stretch. Kneel down on hands and knees. Slowly raise your arm and swing it under your body, reaching as far as possible along your upper back. Do the same thing on the opposite side. Start with four repetitions and gradually work up to ten or fifteen.

Another exercise for the later stages of postpartum is the half sit-up. Lie back with your knees bent and feet flat on the floor. Stretch arms and hands out toward your legs and lift your shoulders and upper body until you can touch one leg. Lie back and repeat on the opposite side. Begin with four repetitions daily and gradually increase to ten per session.

Here's an excellent exercise to strengthen your abdomen and lower back, though again it should not be performed until a few weeks after delivery. Lie back on the floor with your knees bent. Make sure your spine is pressed flat against the floor. Then lift your knees slowly until you can clasp them with your hands and pull them to your chest. Hold that position for a few seconds, then relax. Begin with four repetitions, and work up to ten per session.

WAIST

Stand with your feet eight to ten inches apart and balance your weight equally on both feet. Raise one arm overhead while stretching the opposite arm as far as you can down your leg (but do not rest your weight against your leg). Keep hands, fingers, and shoulders relaxed. Begin with five on each side and gradually increase to fifteen per session. You may attempt this exercise as soon as you feel comfortable after delivery.

Table 12:1 HEART RATE GUIDELINES FOR POSTPARTUM EXERCISE

| | Beats per minute | |
Age	Limit	Maximum
20	150	200
25	146	195
30	142	190
35	138	185
40	135	180
45	131	175

Each figure represents 75 percent of the maximum heart rate that would be predicted for the corresponding age group. Under proper medical supervision, more strenuous activity and higher heart rates may be appropriate.
Reprinted from ACOG Home Exercise Programs, 1985.

POSTURE

Whenever you get out of bed, stretch your spine. Set shoulders back and down and balance weight on both feet. Walk straight and tall, with your buttocks tucked in.

■ *A Final Recommendation*

Although exercise can offer many pluses, mothers may already be getting plenty of exercise just by caring for their baby and/or other children and should take special care to begin exercising slowly and increase intensity level gradually. Also keep in mind that there are wide variations in the amount and intensity of exercise that each new mother can do. We recommend consulting with your physician in order to develop an individualized, closely monitored exercise program that will keep you safe and allow you to achieve maximum health benefits as well.

INDEX